CLEVELAND INDIANS
FACTS & TRIVIA

by
Marc Davis

The E. B. Houchin Company
est. 1992

South Bend, Indiana

The E. B. Houchin Company
23700 Marquette Blvd. A-8
South Bend, Indiana 46628

ISBN: 0-938313-25-8

First Printing: May 1997

Cover photo by Torry Names
Collector's cards from author's private collection

Printed in USA

Table of Contents

For

My Grandpa Tomsic

*the #1 Indians fan
in the world.*

*Thank you for all the
summer memories.*

INTRODUCTION

All right, I'll admit it. Ever since I read a book about Pete Rose, I've been a sworn Reds fan. On afternoons that Cincinnati played the Cubbies on WGN, I would run home from school to catch the last half of the game. It was a real thrill for a boy to watch his heroes play a game he always dreamed he would be playing on TV one day. I wish I had an old diamond war story to tell, about how my once shining career was ruined by an injury, but the fact of the matter is, I never was more than an adequate infielder who made life miserable for first basemen. Not that I wasn't any good, or even athletic. Hey, I have to reserve some dignity. It's just that my aspirations of being like Bench or Concepcion always remained a dream.

Oh, how I loved that dream. Sometimes, I still recall it, and I know deep down inside that I would have been an All-Star shortstop for the Reds in some alternate reality or other. (Sorry, Barry Larkin. In the dream, I had a stronger arm and hit for a higher average. Plus, I usually finished in the 40-home run range per season.) Unfortunately, lucrative contracts have no real substance in dreams, but, oh, well.

Then 1990 came and the Reds won the World Series. I was in heaven. I walked through the world with a sauntering step of pride. Everything seemed perfect. It was about that same time that Cleveland was struggling to keep out of the American League East cellar. Ohio had the best team in baseball and one of the worst.

So why write a book about the Indians? That's easy.

Over the years, my baseball allegiance has expanded to northern Ohio. For one thing, my grandfather who lives in Ashtabula, about an hour and a half drive from Jacobs Field, is a devout Tribe follower. I have spent numerous summer vacations at my grandparents' house, and there was always a TV set or a radio placed on a table in the backyard so we could keep track of how the Indians were doing that day, which, of course, usually meant they were losing. Still, it was not long before I began considering Cleveland as my favorite American League team. Through those fond memories, I have recollected a lot of the moments and players of recent Tribe history.

Second of all, I like rooting for the underdog. Was there ever a team in pro sports that was more of a long shot than the Indians going into the '90s? Then, when they were about to make everyone forget about the seasons of mishap, a higher force ruined their chances. Instead of folding, they rebounded and played even better the next year. The Cleveland Indians are a team of character and strong will. That makes rooting for them easy.

While researching the Indians history then, it was easy to put myself in the shoes of the franchise's most loyal fans throughout the course of their existence. That is the one thing writers can do. We can see out of someone else's eyes and interpret their hearts. In a way it allows me to get sentimental about moments that may have otherwise been before my time. It also allows me to understand what it means to be an Indians fan, now and before.

As Bill Clinton has said a dozen times, and with a straight face, too: "I feel your pain."

Of course, I could also add that I feel your excitement, your delight. And your love for a proud organization.

CLEVELAND INDIANS FACTS & TRIVIA

JUST THE FACTS

1
The Dog Days
of Summer

You could find the ghost of Ivan Pavlov in the nose bleed section of Cleveland Stadium every time the Indians lost during the 1960s, '70s and those dreadful '80s. He had season tickets.

I know this because baseball in Cleveland once had its own version of the "Dawg Pound", only it was a less brutal and far less antagonizing place for the opposition to visit. Actually, that's D-O-G, as in: "*Boy, our baseball team is a real dog.*" A sentiment echoed repeatedly by fans throughout most of the second half of the 20th Century.

During the seventh inning stretch, you could even see a transparent, pale image of Pavlov ringing a bell.

Every summer the whimpering from the Indians faithful grew louder, and, even though Roseanne never sang the National Anthem in Cleveland, the yelps of frustration became more and more prominent as the team continuously dug themselves deeper in the standings, usually before August. Their chances were buried like a favorite bone beneath the infield dirt.

Fans would go home season after season starving like ... well, like wayward dogs. There was so much salivating that Pavlov found the Stadium bleachers an ideal place to conduct posthumous follow-ups to his famous experiment on conditioned reflexes. Often you would hear the crack of an opponent's bat and watch the ball sail over the leftfield fence. Then there would be the annoying chime of a dinner bell.

Ring. Ring.

40 summers of discontent. 40 seasons without as much as a single post-season contest.

Just how bad has it been?

About as bad as an off-key Broadway comedy. Sometimes it was embarrassing to watch, and the jokes (usually slung after the games) were about as funny as banging your knee on the coffee table in the middle of the night. After their appearance in the 1954 World Series, the Indians finished in fourth place or lower 35 times prior to the memorable '95 campaign. *35!* (That's not a typo, folks.) At least that always left room for improvement.

Cleveland Stadium was the only place in Baseball where the fans left the game early to hit the showers. As they vacated their seats, the faint sound of a bell would reach their ears again.

Ring. Ring.

About as bad as a sore thumb that keeps getting in the way when you try to perform simple tasks, such as smashing the radio when the broadcaster's voice conspiriatorially rises: "Another fly ball, deep to left field. It's gone... the Red Sox win." Or the Yankees win. Or whatever team the Tribe played that day. You have to live with that sore thumb and try your darndest to avoid bumping it and reminding yourself how painful it is. You try to pamper it by placing it in a splint and hope it will get better with time. 40 years is a heck of a long time to have a sprained thumb.

And yet, through the static of your busted radio, you could still hear that ringing.

About as bad as "Taking Care of Business" being played over and over on every station across Ohio. The thing about the Indians when they were perennial doormats was you heard about it wherever you went. Walk in for a haircut and the barber would tell you that his softball team could win more games with the Tribe's schedule. Go to the bar for a gin and tonic and the bartender, in between popping caps off beer bottles, would divulge that Cleveland's pitching was as woeful as his love life. The gas station attendant had his own complaints to register. So did the librarian. Heck, even the plumber who couldn't fix your pipes would tell you how the Indians were messing up. People weren't happy at the ball park, so they made your life miserable away from it. And you already knew the Indians were baseball's version of the skinny kid getting his milk money taken from him.

Besides, the bell jingling in the bleachers was reminder enough.

Ring ...

About as bad as a Pauly Shore movie. No matter how long you stayed and tried to watch, it kept getting worse and worse. If you didn't walk out half way through, after it was over you vowed never to see another one. Not even for free on TV. Maybe you even tried to get a refund for the price of your ticket.

Ring ...

You get the point.

But as any loyal fan will attest, there was more to the Indians than losing. There were foot long hot dogs and crackerjacks. You usually had your pick of seats. And there were the memories of a foregone past illuminating from a once proud dugout. No, the tribe wasn't always that bad. In contrast to the team's lower finishes in the standings, over the long haul of nearly a hundred seasons, their won-loss record would reflect a different sentiment entirely. Throughout its history, the club has maintained a winning percentage over .500.

If we thought about the history of the franchise, we'd remember Nap Lajoie, Tris Speaker, and Bob Feller. Or we'd read about them, and a smile would come over our faces. Then we'd realize: "Boy, Cleveland had some great teams." And we would think of the future. Someday, Cleveland will have another great team.

Well, the future was ushered in by a towering blast from Albert Belle's bat, or Manny Ramirez's bat, or Jim Thome's. Skyscraper-type shots put out at Jacobs Field that elicited the waking up of sellout crowds, the healing of time's wounds, and the celebrations of a hundred victories. But the best part of all is that we can't hear that annoying dinner bell amid all the bomb-bursting fireworks and the hurricane of cheering and whistling and foot stomping that rocks the grandstands.

No, I believe the ghost of Pavlov no longer has that bell. He traded it in for a blow horn so he too can root the Indians to victory.

2
The Prior Aliases
of Chief Wahoo

Okay. So maybe you never knew Chief Wahoo had something in common with the legendary John Wayne. Sure he starred in his own motion picture, *Major League*, but that's not what I'm talking about. And it isn't that he was once a rugged, hard-boiled tough guy who didn't like getting pushed around, whether it be the marshal, an ornery outlaw or a damsel in distress doing the pushing. No. It's all in the name.

Though he never seems to age, Chief Wahoo has been around a long time. Stitched on caps and uniforms, manufactured on bumper stickers, painted on beer glasses, his features have rarely changed. Of course, sooner or later, he may have to undergo some sort of reconstructive surgery. I mean, let's face it. Nowadays, Chief Wahoo is about as politically correct as Howard Stern. Critics in Cleveland have gone as far in their protest to post billboards featuring the Indians logo along with the message: "Smile For Racism."

Ouch! That's not very good for the image. Still, for better or worse, despite the objections the logo remains as the figurative soul of a Major

League Baseball team.

But he wasn't always Chief Wahoo. Here, let me explain.

Movie stars have a penchant for altering their names. They have about as much regard for changing who they are as us "regular" guys have for changing a flat tire. In order to get anywhere, it has to be done. Take Marion Morrison for instance. He changed his name to John Wayne so he wouldn't be confused for the cavalry commander's love interest.

As for ol' Chief Wahoo?

I guess the only criteria for a sports team would be choosing a name that doesn't invoke the image of a bunch of sissies running around in hoop skirts. Sometimes, just like in the Land-of-Make-Believe, the situation calls for an identity check. For instance, the Cleveland baseball team we have come to know and love and root for until our voices go on strike have not always been the Indians. No. By all accounts, the Cleveland Indians have been "reinvented" a total of four times throughout its life span.

In order to trace the lineage of the team's nicknames, we must first go back to the inception of the American League in 1900. To a time when Chief Wahoo was a Bluebird.

It all started with one man's vision of improving the grand old game of baseball. For Byron Bancroft "Ban" Johnson, forming a second major league in professional baseball was more akin to a child he would adopt and raise into adulthood than it was to America following it's own destiny. After all, it took a strong influence to mold the National Pastime into the shape it resembles today, and Johnson proved to be an aggressor. Since 1893, he had served as president of the Western League, a circuit that fielded minor league ball clubs from the Midwest. It was a small organization compared to the Goliath of baseball, the National League. Founded in 1876, thus earning the title "Senior Circuit", the NL survived the last quarter of the century as pro baseball's major league mainstay.

With the advent of the NL reducing its stable from 12 teams to eight in 1900, Johnson recognized an opportunity to break the monopoly. He moved teams to some of the vacated NL cities, including putting one each in Cleveland, Washington, and Baltimore, and going into direct competition with the NL in Chicago. Since the boundaries of his league had expanded, Johnson re-christened his loop the American League.

Feeling a little threatened by these maneuvers, the NL made a deal with him. They agreed to recognize the AL, only if it remained a minor league in 1900. That was fine with the upstart president. It gave his teams an opportunity to form local followings.

Johnson did not declare his circuit to be a major league until one year later, and 1901 is considered to be both the actual birth year of the American League and the beginning of the modern era of professional baseball. This progression came after the AL expanded further eastward by staking claims amid NL territory in Philadelphia and Boston. Johnson's willingness to cater to players' demands and promise superior financial stability set off an all-out player war that saw many established stars of the day jumping ship to join the infant league. In all, 111 players swapped allegiance and played for Johnson in the first year of the new century.

After two more seasons of raiding National League rosters, the AL proved to be a worthy adversary. In an effort to eliminate further player defections, the NL struck an accord with Johnson. Although the two leagues did not negotiate a merger, the new peace settlement paved the way for the crowning glory in all of sports, the World Series. The first Fall Classic succeeded the 1903 season and was resumed two years later.

Time Out:

The Series of '04 was never played due to the NL champion New York Giants refusing to play the AL champion Boston Somersets. At that time, the post-season match-up was contingent on both teams agreeing to play one another. The only other year the series was canceled was in 1994, due to the players' strike.

Time In:

So in the span of three full seasons, the resolute Johnson achieved what he had set out to do. Both leagues were now on equal ground. Of course, this would not have happened at all if Johnson had proceeded in this venture alone.

Two of the men Johnson counted on to aid his fledgling league with financial backing were Cleveland natives John F. Kilfoyl, proprietor of a men's clothing store, and Charles W. Somers, who had become a millionaire by forming a partnernership with his father in the coal industry. Both men were slightly over the age of thirty. Johnson viewed their youthful vigor as a plus, especially if he was going to be engaged in a long fight with the NL. After meeting with the league president, the two accepted his proposal to become owners of the former Western League Grand Rapids franchise, subsequently relocated to Cleveland in 1900. Somers in particular proved to be more than just a springboard for his own club. His generosity kept franchises in Philadelphia, St. Louis, and Boston going strong at a time when the teams were financially crippled. In fact, spending money, specifically on his own team, was never one of Somers' shortcomings. Because of this, the Cleveland Base Ball Club was able to lure some of the Game's top players early on to come to Ohio.

One task that troubled the Cleveland owners was the selection of a nickname that would honor the valor of the team's players as they took to the ball fields, with wooden bats swinging and horsehide balls flinging, to battle more proudly named teams. Their initial choice: Bluebirds. It didn't take long before the issue of modifying that representation spilled onto the diamond, probably provoking more meetings than necessary at the pitcher's mound.

Okay. Maybe it wasn't quite that big of a dilemma. Whatever way the players may have reacted, fortunately the nickname was changed before the completion of the 1900 season, before the AL became a major league and before Cleveland could be considered an official charter member. In tribute to the color of their uniforms, and, to a lesser extent, reminiscent of the former NL and American Association squads of the same name, the moniker was shortened to Blues.

The AL Cleveland franchise played its first true season with this name, but it still failed to conjure up the image of machismo the players wanted. So, for the 1902 season, the team unveiled another new identity. The rest of the league now referred to them as the Bronchos.

Of course, that wasn't quite right either.

The following season, the Clevelanders called themselves the Naps. Not naps, as in an afternoon rest session. These weren't a bunch of cranky three year old impersonators whining about not making enough millions, a.k.a., the majority of today's professional athletes. Naps, as in Napoleon Lajoie, the team's second baseman and one of the game's first living legends.

Nap Lajoie. (It's pronounced *la-ZHWAH*, not Laj-a-way as Tommie Lee Jones mockingly says it in his portrayal of Ty Cobb in the movie about the Detroit Tigers legend.) He was considered a defensive genius for his inspired efforts in tracking down any ball within range, and was the fiercest hitter of the dead ball era. A number that reflects this belief is his home run total of 1901. That year he swatted 14 long balls. Most Major Leaguers were on a power trip if they connected on five in a season. More impressive though was his lifetime batting average of .339.

This time it had been the fans who decided the club's identity, through a contest conducted by the *Cleveland Press*. None of the other suggestions that received votes in the poll came close to typifying the spirit of the team. After all, Lajoie's sudden success played a key role in the growth of pro baseball in the area.

He arrived in Cleveland in the spring of 1902, one year removed from the single greatest batting exhibition in the history of the American League. As a Philadelphia Athletic, Lajoie did not merely put on a clinic, he wrote the preface to the book on the art of hitting a baseball by posting a .422 average during the AL's inaugural season.

Time Out:

As is the case with some statistics of the early days, a discrepancy exists for Lajoie's '01 average. Most sources clarify the .422 average, while *Total Baseball*, touted as the Official Encyclopedia of Major League Baseball, contests the actual number is .426. Arguments can be made to support both sides, but here we'll go with the majority of references and accept .422 as the legitimate number. So that means only one player has ever hit for a higher single season average. Rogers Hornsby of the NL St. Louis Cardinals batted .424 in 1924.

Time In:

Lajoie's bat was as unique as his style of fielding. Manufactured by the J.F. Hillerich Company, its dual knobbed handle resulted in a ton of doubles and slashing line drives placed almost at will. His hitting prowess can best be realized when considering one of the few times he was offered an intentional walk but instead swung one-handed and smashed the ball in the gap for extra bases.

Baseball became a passion for Lajoie while he was growing up in Woonsocket, Rhode Island. Early legends he discovered at that time, including King Kelly, Cap Anson, and Hoss Radbourn, inspired him to try out the semi-pro circuit in his hometown. From there, he signed a contract with Fall River of the New England minor leagues where he hit .429 in 80 games. That was how long it took him to land a spot on the National League Philadelphia Phillies in 1897. There he was paid the maximum salary of $2,400 a year, or the amount Barry Bonds makes in the time it takes him to knock the dirt from his cleats. Four seasons later, having gained the reputation of an elite player, Lajoie jumped leagues, without as much as boarding a single train to travel to a neighboring city.

There was one problem with Lajoie playing for the rival AL Philadelphia Athletics. At the start of the 1902 campaign, the Phillies successfully sought a court order that restricted their former star from playing with any other baseball team in the city. The block had been attempted the previous season, but Lajoie, claiming that the injunction interfered with his constitutional rights, won the first court battle and was cleared to play for Connie Mack's Athletics. The State Supreme court overturned the ruling the next spring, concluding Nap's career in Philly and forcing Mack to trade him to a safe haven outside the Pennsylvania courts' jurisdiction. So he ended up in Cleveland. The only catch was that the second baseman would sit out when his new team played the Athletics in Philadelphia. The quarrel subsided entirely when the NL agreed to recognize the AL as a valid major league.

All this behind the scenes dispute did was bring the best player of the day to a town with a franchise that desperately needed definition. By September of 1904, Nap was promoted to the rank of player-manager.

After posting a record slightly below .500 in his first full year in this dual capacity, he led the team to four winning seasons. On August 17, 1909, with the team sputtering to the point where the local media began referring to Lajoie's squad as the "Napkins", he resigned his managerial duties in order to concentrate on playing full-time again. One incident that may have helped him decide to step down happened in 1907.

George Stovall, the Naps' fiery first baseman, struck his manager with a chair. The reason? Lajoie had dropped him down in the batting order. Bickering among his players aside, Nap maintained a fully loaded lineup during his stint at the helm.

During his post-managerial days, he strung together a series of remarkable seasons, hitting over .360 three straight years and .335 in another. In his final year in a Cleveland uniform, his batting average slipped to .258. After Nap's departure (back to the Athletics, ironically) following the dismal season of 1914, another new nickname was needed.

The *Cleveland Press* conducted another poll and this time the team was dubbed the Indians. The fan responsible for the winning entry said he chose the name in tribute to the legacy of the Major League's first Native American ball player. Though it was common practice at the start of the century, Cleveland remains the only major league team to still be named after a player. The honoree: Louis Sockalexis. Never heard of him? He never played for the AL Cleveland team. His tour of fame began when he joined the Cleveland Spiders of the National League in 1897. His smart hitting and agility in right field, along with a powerful, precise arm quickly made him a crowd favorite. In 94 games from 1897-99, he collected a total of 115 hits and 55 RBIs, while posting a .313 average. It was a meteoric demise for the Penobscot tribesman, hastened by frequent clashes with the bottle. He played in only seven games his final season in the big leagues. Still, Cleveland fans did not forget him.

Use of the new title was initially deemed temporary while the team played out the 1915 season. Over the years, as ownership changed hands from time to time, another transition in name was seldom pursued. Despite the criticisms that use of the nickname, the logo, and the actions of fanatics in the stands—with their painted faces, tomahawk chops, war whoops, Indian chief impersonations, etc.—were encouraging racial clichés, the name has "lived long and prospered" as the great Vulcan philosopher Spock would say. Of course, I don't know that Spock would necessarily agree with a baseball team calling themselves the Vulcans and having a mascot with long, pointy ears continuously holding his hand up in a V-shape either.

Well, for good or for worse, the Indians have kept the name. Through good seasons and horrible seasons, Chief Wahoo remains as much a part of the team as the players beneath the caps. Those old enough to do so might remember him featured every morning on the *Cleveland Plain Dealer*, smiling as usual, two fingers raised in a victory salute to inform the many readers of a hard fought win the night before, or, in the case of defeat, sporting a bruised eye and missing some teeth. Today, he is featured on billboards.

John Wayne had to change his name so he could become famous. Chief Wahoo may have to change his again in order to protect the innocent.

3

The Great Automobile Race

Most of the players on the field that day had faced him before, earlier in the year, in season's past, and knew that when Napoleon LaJoie stood at the plate, sizing them up, taking aim with a slow, measured practice swing, it was an authentic warning to "watch your knee caps, boys." Playing defense against the big Frenchman was like looking down the barrel of a loaded gun, held by an itchy trigger finger. And old Nap, he knew this as he locked the bat above his shoulder, waiting to uncoil, a slight autumn breeze fanning the perspiration that slid down his face. He could read it in the pitcher's eyes, in the eyes of the entire infield. It was the cold stare of caution, the St. Louis Browns rocking back on their heals in anticipation of a bullet line drive. First they'd hear the splitting crack of the bat—nobody else's bat made that sound—then a blazing object would jump out at them, possibly allowing enough time to move, out of sheer reflex, or stab their gloves at it, maybe a little too slow this time. Then they'd hear another crack: the shattering of an ankle; or least of all, the forming of a ball-size lump on the chest.

He could sense this state of mind as he tightened his grip, as if it was being relayed from one infielder to the other. Some powerful energy force that penetrated his own body and pumped his adrenaline. Nap knew he had to be perfect at the plate in this season finale double header if he wanted to overtake Ty Cobb for the batting crown of 1910. He could not afford to take a free pass, or hit into a fielder's choice. Or give himself up for a sacrifice.

So he planted his spikes in the batter's box. He spit out a mouthful of tobacco juice, and leveled his concentration toward the pitcher's wind up. The arm came forward, hurling the ball toward home plate.

Nap stepped forward as he unleashed the bat in a trademark fluid motion that caused the ball to leap like a rabbit out of a brier patch, out of sight and in the clearing before it was spotted again. Hub Northen gave chase, striding toward the descent of the ball. Into the far reaches of center field ...

By all accounts of the day, Tyrus Raymond Cobb—holder of 12 AL batting titles—was the greatest player ever to take the field, but the extent of his spirit was fire wrapped in flesh and bone. He had a rigid scowl when he stepped up to bat, his eyes narrowed to a mad dog stare. An expression that exposed a rabid tooth anxious to take a bite out of an infielder's leg when he ran the bases, the teeth being his sharpened spikes raised to the shin during a hard slide, able to break the skin with the single-mindedness of completing a tactical move in a game of chess.

There was no doubt that the man possessed a mean streak that ran down his back as blatantly as the stripe on a skunk. Everyone who opposed him knew it. Some have chronicled him as the angriest man to ever play the game. Recently, baseball scholars have made a legitimate attempt to see him in a different light, contributing his actions to a life surrounded by the death of loved ones, and a rookie season where he fell victim to a parade of hazing by the Detroit Tiger veterans, treatment that gave Cobb a sour attitude toward fellow ball players. They have also documented the few occasions where he actually benefited man, or donated a portion of his lofty earnings to a charitable cause. The "Georgia Peach" may very well have shown that he had a good nature tucked away somewhere in the shadowy depths of his being, but no matter how often they turn over the legend, no matter how many different angles they inspect it, Cobb will always be remembered as a demon on the diamond.

There are reasons for this infamous acclaim.

He once jumped into the stands to pursue a heckler that had been giving it to him royally for nearly an entire game. The incident occurred during a contest in Bennett Park in the summer of 1910, against New York. That day also happened to be Cobb's return to the Tiger lineup after sitting out two games so he could sulk over a teammate's blown hit-and-run. The spectator, a black man, began to move away from his seat, unwilling to mix it up with the mentally battered ball player. Security subdued Cobb before he was able to reach the man and inflict the world of hurt that was burning in his eyes.

It was not an isolated incident. Today, leaping into the stands by an athlete may be deemed necessary to rob a batter of a home run, or accept the congratulatory embraces of fans, but Ty Cobb's prototype of "reaching out to the ticket holders" was an attempt to frighten and bewilder. Two years after the Bennett Park affair, the "Georgia Peach" was at it again. A regular Cobb heckler, situated 12 rows behind the Tiger bench in New York's Hilltop Park, insisted on berating him before the start of a game against the Highlanders (soon to be known as the Yankees) and continuously slung verbal assaults about him and his family for three innings. Reaching his boiling point, Ty scaled the grandstands with the crazed, bloodthirsty agility of a professional wrestler diving back into the ring with a folded chair in hand. The spectator this time was a crippled man named Claude Leuker, who had only two fingers, both on the same hand. The Tiger outfielder bulldozed fans on the way up, and when he reached the man, he pummeled him with flying fists, then kicked and stomped on him. Those witnessing the horror screamed at Cobb to show some mercy. Finally, an umpire and stadium security were able to break up the melee.

He may have helped win, or been the sole provider of numerous wins for the Tigers over the long haul of his career, but he alienated himself from his teammates in the process. Sitting next to him on the bench would have been like standing in a cage with a temperamental gorilla. (The one that beats up the suitcase in those old TV ads). The slightest of comments taken the wrong way or the simplest of miscues could detonate him, so it was easiest for the other players to keep their distance. The fights he did pick with opponents, teammates or even umpires, usually waged after games beneath the grandstands, are now a legendary part of the lore of his playing days. He was also the target of numerous, hand-scripted death threats from fans around the country.

It was easy to hate Cobb, and still is today. Besides, he was one of the earliest practitioners of a now time honored tradition, the pre-season holdout.

If someone would have held a mirror to Ty Cobb, the reverse image would have been that of Napoleon Lajoie's. At six foot-one, Larry, as he was sometimes called, had the good looks that was of the same mold as the classic film stars that soon would become popular—say, John Gilbert with the derring-do of Douglas Fairbanks in an upper body that seemed to be concrete slabs beneath a baggy jersey. Adored in the stadiums and streets by young fans who hoped to be like him someday and admired by their parents, he was the spitting image of what a sports hero should be. Comrades and opponents respected and emulated him as well. Nobody, except *maybe* Cobb, disliked Larry.

Time Out:

In fact, when Ty made out his all-time greatest players list, somewhere around 1945, he excluded his rival. That might just mean that he didn't believe Nap to be as good as he appeared to be, but he'd be the only one.

Time In:

So, Lajoie was much more popular than Cobb. He was a veteran on his way down the slope of greatness. Cobb, on the other hand was only 25 at the time, the eccentric hotshot who had all ready grabbed his fair share of individual glory. Not many wanted him to retain the batting title for a fourth consecutive year in 1910. Only the most loyal Tiger supporters and those who put money on him were rooting for the "Georgia Peach."

From the beginning of time, throughout the annals of history, battles have been waged between good and evil. Audiences are suckers for a good hero versus villain plot.

That was the American League batting crown race of 1910 in a nutshell. Lajoie vs. Cobb. Good against bad.

In the time it took the outfielder to turn around and adjust to the trajectory of the ball, he seemingly lost it, as if the sky above Sportsman's Park had transformed into an imposing blind spot. Rounding first base, Nap saw the ball soar beyond the limp glove of Hub Northen, so he increased speed. He was going for a triple. Applause rang from the grandstands as he pulled up at third base, the ball just then skipping onto the infield.

On his next trip to the plate, Nap noticed something different in the Browns' defensive alignment. Red Corriden, a rookie third baseman, fidgeted on the rim of the grass beyond the infield dirt. He crouched, his glove resting close to his body.

Nap hunched his shoulders and squared the bat in front of him as the pitch came in. The fat of the wood popped, vibrating the muscle of his palms, and the ball skidded forward. It was not a particularly good bunt. Shortstop Bobby Wallace broke late on the ball, but it continued rolling until he reached down and scooped it off the infield lawn.

No longer could he sprint down the chalk line. It was more of a furious gallop now. But when he pounced on the bag with a heavy squish, *Nap could see a stream of arms being thrown into the air behind the first base foul line. He had beaten out the throw.*

Two for two.

With Corriden still playing deep his next time at bat, Nap legged out another bunt single that he dragged down the third base side. Since he did not get a good jump on the ball, Corriden could only let it roll to a stop, pick it up and toss it back to the pitcher.

His fourth plate appearance resulted in a replay of the previous time: a sloppy bunt heading toward the laid back third baseman. This time as Nap ran down the line, a majority of the crowd cheered the inevitable. There was the sound of his shoe smacking the bag, and the first baseman pulled away empty handed.

Four for four.

Done as a promotional stunt, the Chalmers Automobile Company announced at the beginning of the season that they would be awarding new cars to the National and American League batting champions. The model offered was a Chalmers 30, one heck of a bonus for a ball player at that time. Such a prestigious reward made for a stretch run of intense drama. It became as coveted as a prominent purse in a prize fight. Both the Naps and the Tigers had sputtered, so the race between Cobb and Lajoie became a main event by mid-summer. Fans suddenly became as aware of the battle for the Chalmers automobile as they were of the pennant races.

In September, it appeared that Cobb's bid for the automobile would come up short. Trailing Lajoie by eight points, he missed a total of 10 games due to an inflammation of the optic nerves in his left eye. Included in that stretch of games were two widely heralded series with the Naps, one series at home and the other on the road. Cleveland newspapers printed cracks about Mean Mr. Cobb having turned chicken. The ailment affected him enough to the point that he wore smoked glasses on the days he missed.

Being the great clutch hitter that he was, Cobb quickly made up the difference when he returned to the lineup. After going on a hitting binge in the final week of the season, he took what appeared to be an insurmountable cushion. In a move that was again ridiculed as an act of cowardice, the Tiger outfielder sat out his team's final two games in order to protect his position as the leading hitter in the league.

Cobb thought for sure the Chalmers automobile was his.

Following another bunt hit his first at bat in the second game of the double header—now, he was an incredible five for five—Nap Lajoie stepped into the batter's box to a cavalcade of applause, as well as some guttural boos. A portion of the fans began chanting objections, and they waved their hands in frustration at the way the home team seemed to lay down every time he came to the plate. Once again the void down the third base side extended to the outfield grass. He contemplated the situation: runner on first, Corriden's hands relaxed at his side, his stance sluggish. Cobb's lofty lead was evaporating. This was no time for delusions. He squared to bunt.

The pitcher's arm came forward in a windmill motion. It was a mild offering, located in the meat of the strike zone. All Nap had to do was hold the bat over the plate, then slap at the ball and he was speeding off toward first.

He put a little too much wood on it. The ball hopped down the third base side, into the glove of a slowly advancing Corriden. In the instant it took him to pivot and try a throw, the rookie bobbled the ball. Cheers and shouts of contempt erupted at once as Nap crossed the bag.

In the press box, the official scorer stared down at the field, to mull over the play he had just witnessed.

"Lajoie outguessed us," St. Louis Browns manager, Jack O' Connor would tell reporters following the conclusion of the double-header "He beat us at our own game."

Call it a battle of wills then, right? "Peach Pie" O' Connor, as he was often called, continued, saying it would have been unwise to sacrifice his rookie's body by positioning him up close when the Cleveland second baseman attempted to bunt. Lajoie could pull back his swing, smack the ball and ruin the boy's smile.

A perfect excuse? Not hardly. As evidenced by his performance that day, Nap had never been a crafty bunter. Nobody would have expected him to mess up his own swing by faking a bunt just to lure his opposition in. Nobody would have expected him to try and safely execute a bunt for a hit, either.

That is, unless the defense gave him a ton of real estate to try it on.

In defense of his actions, Corriden admitted he was ordered to play back. He also echoed his manager's philosophy of safety first, get the out later, when he added: "I wasn't going to get killed playing in on Lajoie."

The umpire calling the double-header, Billy Evans, agreed. In his report to American League president, Ban Johnson, filed days later, he wrote it was his opinion that the Browns' measures were strictly cautionary and not intended to aid Lajoie in any way.

Others, of course, saw it differently.

After a while, E. V. Parish knew how to score the play. With the runner on first breaking and advancing on a bunt executed to the left side, it came down to a basic rule of thumb. He made his decision, jotted it down for the records.

Moments after he made his ruling, Parish noticed someone approaching him. It was the Browns' assistant coach, "Handsome" Harry Howell. Parish was not surprised to see him. It had been somewhat of a circus all day long, with representatives from both clubs showing interest in his rulings.

Howell leaned forward and asked how he scored the play.

Parish glanced at him. "Lajoie moved the lead runner over on a bunt. I had to give him a sacrifice. That means it was not an official at bat. I charged an error to your guy for bobbling the ball."

Howell leaned in further. He asked if--or, rather suggested that Parish change it to a hit. "Nap has been beating out bunts all day long," he said. "He had this one beat just as easily."

The scorekeeper shook his head. "He has to earn a hit before I give it to him."

Later in the game, a St. Louis bat boy came by and handed him a piece of paper. He unfolded it and read the message:

Mr. Parish: If you can see where Lajoie gets a B.H. instead of a sacrifice, I will give you an order for a forty dollar suit of clothes--for sure. Answer by boy. In behalf of_____, I ask it of you.

Folding up the paper again, E. V. Parish steadied his gaze toward the field.

It was never determined whether or not St. Louis manager O'Connor and his aide Howell were paid off to help fix the batting race that year. Or if it was a case of a scar cutting too deeply into their psyches. A scar inflicted by Tyrus Cobb.

Whatever their reasoning, the fact that the St. Louis Browns were feeding Napoleon Lajoie hits on October 9, 1910 did not go unnoticed.

Entering the season finale assured of eighth place, O'Connor and his team had nothing to lose. One would have thought that they would not want to compromise their dignity, or the credibility of baseball, but the human mind cannot always be understood. Their actions were especially obvious to E. V. Parish, a local sportswriter who, as the official score-keeper of the twin bill, was in a position to play god of the baseball world, so to speak, and help Nap steal the title for certain. Instead, he kept his integrity intact by ruling with an honest pen.

One other person who was onto the fix was Hugh Fullerton, a fellow sportswriter who soon would become a key figure in determining the outcome of the Great Automobile Race.

Nap beat out two more bunts in the second game. On his final plate appearance, most of the faithful at Sportsman's Park roared in euphoria, as if he alone held the club of crucifixion over the beaten, deplorable body of Ty Cobb. He tightened his grip and lowered the bat to meet the ball, dropping another bunt into play.

The laid back defense reacted slowly once again. Nap kicked up dirt, dust and chalk. With his back to the play, he did not know if the ball was heading to first base in an attempt to get there before him. He leaped for the bag.

The umpire waved his arms. "Safe."

Eight official at bats in the two games. Eight hits.

Following the conclusion of the twin bill, fans poured onto the field. They ran up to Napoleon, reached out to pat him on the shoulders. They congratulated him for winning the batting title.

Ty Cobb overtaken by a valiant effort in the waning moments of the race? Not exactly.

Headlines may not always be accurate. Ask Thomas Dewey about that. Such was the case with some national newspapers on the morning of October 10, 1910, when they so triumphantly declared: "Lajoie Defeats Cobb."

The majority of sports columnists who figured Lajoie had reached the magic number needed to win the batting title, took vast liberties in describing the affairs at Sportsman's Park the day before. Some only hinted at the Browns' reluctance to field his "ingenious" bunts. Others blatantly cried foul, saying St. Louis rolled over and played dead so he could have his way. The *St. Louis Post* even went so far as to suggest that the Browns owed Mr. Cobb a Chalmers automobile. Most were in agreement that O'Connor's and Howell's actions gave a black eye to the face of the game. One exception was the *Cleveland Plain Dealer*, which attempted to add respectability to the Potent-Bat-Scares-Fielder theory, by claiming a sound defense always plays deep when facing the fiercest hitter in the game.

There were a few publications, such as the *Sporting News*, that had the "Georgia Peach" slightly edging out the big Frenchman. All the predictions, of course, were unofficial. So, if anything, the outcome was clouded with uncertainty. American League president, Ban Johnson had the final say on the numbers, but before he took on the task, Hugh Fullerton decided to alter destiny.

A native of New York, Fullerton had been in the press box with E. V. Parish the day of the double-header. During mid-summer, he had accepted the job of co-scorekeeper at a Tigers game. In that contest, he originally awarded a base hit to Cobb on a questionable play. His partner overruled the call, arguing that the fielder involved in the play should have been able to field the ball cleanly. The hit was changed to an error. In an attempt to even the deal for Cobb, Fullerton found the records of that game and changed the error back to a hit. He then submitted the alteration to Johnson, claiming Cobb had been unfairly duped by his partner.

This minor correction helped tip the scale. When Johnson released the official numbers on October 15, Cobb had come out ahead by the finite margin of .384944 to Lajoie's .384084.

Cobb's requiem came after he warded off a personal blow of sorts. Following the season finale, eight of his teammates had allegedly sent his rival a telegram of congratulations for winning the automobile.

For their part in attempting to fix the batting race of 1910, Jack O'Connor and Harry Howell were fired by the St. Louis Browns. (Parish told Johnson that he figured Howell had been the one who attempted to bribe him with the promise of a new wardrobe if he switched Lajoie's sacrifice to a hit. The actual identity of the note's author was never determined.) After the league president finished his own investigation of the conspiracy, the two men were handed a more severe penalty: lifetime banishment from professional baseball. Lajoie and Corriden were dismissed of any wrong doing. In baseball it isn't a crime to take what the defense gives. Nor is it a crime to follow the orders given by your manager.

New data, unearthed over 70 years later, provided pertinent evidence that swayed opinions once more as to who the real batting champion was in 1910. Working as associate editor of *The Sporting News* in 1981, Paul McFarlane decided to recount the hits awarded to both batsmen in every game during that infamous season. He found out that a game in which Cobb had delivered two hits had some how been credited twice in his final statistics. He was awarded two extra hits he never earned.

Despite the mistake, a special committee, headed by baseball's commissioner at the time, Bowie Kuhn, refused to update the official numbers. They believed tampering with a long forgotten issue would only open up more debate. Following up on it's own claim, *The Sporting News Official Record Book* immediately began recognizing Lajoie as the true batting champ of 1910. After all the years, it is still a matter of opinion as to who actually deserved the title.

Maybe Hugh Chalmers was the only one with a proper solution to the mess. In honor of each of their individual accomplishments, and more than likely, as a way to help lick the wounds the game sustained from all the controversy, the president and owner of the company named after him, awarded motor cars to both players. The ceremony took place at Shibe Park, in Philadelphia, prior to the opening game of the World Series that featured Connie Mack's Athletics and the Chicago Cubs. As a way of avoiding similar ordeals in the future, the following year, the Chalmers Auto Company began rewarding batting champions with a Most Valuable Player plaque instead of a car.

So, that's how the Great Automobile Race of 1910 ended in a tie before either participant actually got behind the wheel. Maybe the two of them should have opted for a drag race around the bases in their brand new cars in order to declare a winner once and for all.

Then again, that might not have been such a good idea. Ty Cobb probably would have slashed Lajoie's tires with his spikes and won by forfeit.

4
Buy Me Some Peanuts and ... a New Ball Park

Baseball is our fountain of youth. A fountain we swallow memories from to savor for a lifetime, memories that replenish us as we get older. Everyone can remember hearing their fathers and grandfathers telling dramatic stories about the legends of their day, and reveling in the time of their childhood when they invented their own glory within the friendly confines of a local ball diamond. And who really cared how farfetched the stories may have seemed, or how sentimental, because we were all under the spell of the timelessness of baseball. Everyone can understand this affection. We have all been Boys of Summer (or Girls of Summer) at some time or another, whether it was in little league, sandlot ball or stick ball with parked cars and manhole covers for bases, or even a disorganized resemblance of the game played in a park at a family reunion. Baseball is an institution that transcends age, gender, religion, and our stations in life.

The grand old game itself ages and grows as the years wear on, but its meaning and influence remain forever young at heart. I first saw this in my grandfather's eyes, the effervescent joy that came from winging a baseball, whenever he played catch with his grandsons. And, for the life of him, he *was* as much a nine-year-old, or 11-year-old as me or my brothers. You also see this when you watch your sons and daughters throw a ball around in the back yard, or watch kids chasing fly balls in the park down the street. Just give a kid a ball and a glove, and they've got a friend for life.

Everyone has their own recollections of growing up with the game. Going into the garage to dig out the old mitt at the first sign of spring, or journeying over to the sporting goods store to by a brand new one, with an allowance saved up over the winter; the smell of fresh leather; the romance of oiling it and breaking it in before the first big game. Then waking up on a summer morning, riding your bike to the ball field to meet some friends, glove secured on the handlebars, legs peddling with a renewed urgency and a sense of freedom. Eager to fire in the first pitch, to hear the glorious crack of a crisp base hit. Feeling like the wind as you whip around the bases ... All of this culminating in that magical moment when the ball smacks the pocket of Old Faithful, or the Best New Leather in Town.

I miss those summer afternoons where the biggest concern was that dinner time would come too soon and break up one heck of a game. Oh, to be able to gather our friends right now on the diamond across from the school or the vacant parking lot on Memory Lane, and "play ball!" until the darkness squeezes out the last sight of that old, worn out baseball.

Of course, there's always the solace of attending a Major League game. For just as we remember our own playing days, we can also recall taking trips to the ball park on lazy, summer afternoons. Opening up our hearts to an eye-popping display of clear skies and a green and brown field as bristling and bright as Ray Kinsella's own field of dreams. The ball park is a sacred place. Grownups become children again, skipping out on the tensions of a long day at work to languish in the sun, chew on a hot dog, and holler at the umpires as if they were yelling at their bosses. Children come to dream that someday they will be taking the field, wearing a hometown uniform.

Yes, the ball park is a home away from home.

In Cleveland, that surrogate home is Jacobs Field. Inaugurated April 4, 1994, the Tribe's ball park is a modern-day facility with an old time atmosphere. Naturally, with the team winning, tickets have been hard to come by. This is in sharp contrast to the early '90s, when the organization couldn't give away seats in Municipal Stadium.

My grandfather took my two brothers to a game in the summer of '91. (I couldn't make the trip to my grandparents' that year. Unfortunately, writers sometime have to work "real" jobs, just like every other average Joe.) Looking out across the vast sea of empty seats, my grandpa suggested the three of them try to guess the day's attendance total.

My brother Eric guessed first. Now, you must first be told that Eric has always struggled in math. Any chance he had to sneak a peak at my test paper in class would find him studiously copying from my answers. He thought about it for a moment, then said: "Around 34,520."

"Way too high," Grandpa said with a chuckle.

John, being the eldest brother, but no wiser a mathematician, guessed: "32,500."

"You obviously don't follow the Indians," Grandpa said. Then he began taking a quick count with his finger, acting as if he was tabulating every single head in the Stadium. After a lengthy pause, he declared: "27,100."

They waited through the first half of the seventh inning. Groans came from the crowd after the opposition scored another slew of runs, until finally the third out was made. Then the scoreboard flashed the day's attendance total: 27,101

My brothers looked at Grandpa in amazement. He turned to them with a curious look on his face and laughed. "Darn it. I would have had it exactly, but I forgot to count myself."

Of course, he'd need a computer in his brain to count that fast. His precise "guess" could be attributed to his knowledge of just how his favorite team had been faring lately. Poor play resulted in poor turnouts at Indians home games during the early '90s, so he considered recent attendance totals and formulated his answer according to those numbers.

The team's inability to fill even half the Stadium's capacity on some dates was only one reason Indians ownership began planning to build a new ball park. Cleveland Stadium was also over 60 years old, and had aged more like a man content to become elderly, rather than someone who turns to plastic surgery in an attempt to hide their advancement in years. The few renovations that were done did little to aid it's appearance. Beer cups were often as evident as the people sitting in the paint-chipped seats. Despite efforts to keep the playing surface up to par, infielders were routinely bitten by bad hops. Still, none of these problems forced the Indians to move. For the most part, continuous squabbling over the terms of the team's lease could be blamed.

With a capacity exceeding 74,000, Cleveland Municipal Stadium wasn't constructed for the sole purpose of becoming a baseball team's playing field. City officials hoped its enormous size would enable Cleveland to attract major events, which in turn would increase tourism and bring a financial boost to the city. Over the years, the Stadium has housed auto races, operas, prayer services, musical concerts (including a Beatles invasion in 1966), a circus and other various gatherings. Built near the shore of Lake Erie, a safe distance from public housing and city streets, the Stadium's first "event" was a boxing match on July 3, 1931, between heavyweight champion Max Schmeling and a fighter named Young Stribling. For those interested, the German champ retained his title on a 15th-round technical knockout.

A popular local myth leads many to believe that city officials had a hidden agenda behind their proposal to finance the facility. At the time, it was hoped that construction of a mammoth stadium would persuade the Olympic Committee into selecting Cleveland as the host of the 1932 Summer Games. Jim Toman, author of the book, *Cleveland Stadium: Sixty Years of Memories*, in an article published in *The Plain Dealer* on September 20, 1993, had this to say about the issue: "If it's true, it's never been documented by the Indians, the Browns, the city, or [the Stadium] contractors and it never appears in newspaper clippings." If trying to lure the Olympics to the heartland was the main reason for the Stadium's construction, the ploy proved to be of little consequence. As it turned out, the '32 Games were awarded to the city of Los Angeles.

Contrary to these rumors, Cleveland Stadium was built with the understanding that it would be the home of the Indians. At least, that was what Ernest Barnard, the club's one-time president, had hoped. But, before we are to understand Barnard's motives for providing a baseball team with such a cavernous residence, we must first go back to the beginning of the franchise, when simply finding a place to play was the main concern.

The obvious choice was League Park, the former home of the National League Cleveland franchise known as the Spiders. Built on the corner of Lexington Avenue and East 66th Street after the Spiders previous ball park was destroyed during a thunderstorm, League Park was financed by the team's owner, Frank DeHaas Robison. Opening day was May 1, 1891, and the Spiders played nine consecutive seasons there before they were dropped by the National League. This came after Robison purchased another ball club in St. Louis and was unable to find a buyer for the depleted team he left behind in Cleveland. Actually, depleted wasn't even a good enough description for the state of the Spiders in 1899. After transferring all the quality players from his Cleveland roster to St. Louis, Robison had more or less stripped his original franchise down to the bare bones.

The untimely death of the city's NL team left the playing rights of League Park open for negotiations. Originally, Robison wasn't willing to lease his field to American League competitors. His views quickly changed after John Kilfoyl and Charles Somers, the two men who owned the new AL Cleveland franchise, announced plans to build a new stadium in another part of town. Robison had two options: let his ball park stay virtually dormant while professional baseball moved on in the city, or fatten his bank account by selling the decade old facility. Since he also owned the street car lines that surrounded League Park and foresaw a steady decline in business without baseball in the area, Robison chose to turn the ball park over to Kilfoyl and Somers.

The stadium's design had its peculiarities. For one thing, the right field fence, though it was 40 feet high, was a shallow 290 feet deep. They might as well have put a giant bulls-eye on top of the wall, because home run hitters frequently tried to exploit the unusually short power alley. By comparison, a left field shot would need to travel 375 feet, and maintain a height of 20 feet to reach the bleachers. Pitchers weren't the only ones who despised that right field fence. It was actually a 20-foot wooden base, topped by a 20 foot net that, more times than not, caused unwieldy ricochets. Because of this, right fielders usually had little or no sense of what angle to attack a fly ball from if it looked like it was going to carry to the wall. That's not to say the other two-thirds of the outfield didn't have problems converging on a ball that was destined to carom, especially if the ball bounced off the sets of wooden stairs that occupied the base of the left and center field bleachers. Wooden benches along the foul lines were so close to the field of play that a player had to be careful where he spit his tobacco juice, or a fan would end up with an unsuspected face wash.

Before the season of 1910, League Park needed a makeover. First and foremost, the seating capacity was increased from 9,000 to nearly 21,000. Durable concrete and steel structures took the place of the old wooden grandstands. Also, the foul territory was expanded, so players could chase errant balls without the worry of trampling over spectators. Another change that was intended to aid the defense actually made life more miserable in the shallow depths of right field. The dreaded 20 foot section of wood on the bottom half of the wall was replaced with a 20-foot section of concrete. Unfortunately, they never covered it with padding or handed out crash helmets. They kept the net and its steel support poles above the concrete, as well, leaving one to wonder why they messed with it in the first place. Besides, the alteration failed to reduce the number of balls taken out of the yard.

That short fence became synonymous with the Babe Ruth legend on August 11, 1929. On that day, the "Babe" hit his 500th career home run. Historical significance aside, the best part of the story comes after the ball left the park. Picture yourself as a youngster on that late summer afternoon, maybe missing out on a chance for tickets to the game, or simply not being able to afford them. So, the next best thing is to stand on Lexington Avenue, behind the right field wall, along with a dozen other boys and girls and hope for the chance to chase after a home run. After all, in those days, League Park offered youngsters free admission to a future game if they returned any balls hit onto the street. Picture yourself watching the top of the stadium. You see a ball traveling in a monstrous arc, over your head, and you run … You chase it all the way across the street, a flock of other ball hunters at your heels. Then you find it, resting in a patch of lawn, and you hold it up. It shines in the sun like a prized jewel, but you could never in your life imagine holding such a precious souvenir. Not a Babe Ruth home run, though you may have dreamed about it …

What could be better than owning a Babe Ruth home run ball? Nothing, except returning the memento and meeting the legend in person, shaking his hand and being his honorary guest the next day. The kid who retrieved the ball was given a reward of $20, and an opportunity to sit in the visiting Yankees dugout. Ruth also autographed a baseball for him.

A primary example of the magic of baseball.

The name of the stadium changed to Dunn Field in 1916, in honor of the team's owner at the time, James C. "Sunny Jim " Dunn. The name remained in use for a few years after Dunn's death in 1922, then changed back to League Park. Shortly after the tragedy, at the urging of Dunn's widow, Edith, Ernest Barnard took over the day to day operations of the franchise. During his tenure as president of the Indians, Barnard formed the opinion that League Park wasn't an adequate enough stadium for a major league baseball club. He envisioned a 60,000 seat facility to accommodate the team's growing fan base. Also, since he knew he would be taking over as president of the American League in 1927, Barnard was in a must-sell situation. A larger, more modern complex would present the Indians as a better investment to potential buyers.

Preliminary plans on a stadium proposal were underway when Barnard sold the club, on November 17, 1927. His efforts carried over to the new ownership, which was a syndicate of local businessmen headed by Alva Bradley. Approval for the new stadium, to be financed with city bonds, came one year later.

Building Cleveland Stadium was the task of the Osborn Engineering Company, the same group that served as the renovators of League Park over 20 years before. Their expertise and experience in designing ball parks, so they claimed in various advertisements of the day, allowed them to provide every fan with a full, unobstructed view of the diamond. In truth, there were many spots in the Stadium where a spectator's view was at least partially blocked, such as the foul posts, or the numerous columns that wound around the perimeter of the grandstands.

Throughout its existence as the Indians home, Cleveland Stadium was a pitcher's park. Part of the reason for this was the distance of the fences. The foul posts were 322 feet from home plate. Straight away center field, originally at 470 feet, was baseball's Death Valley. Hitting one out to the deepest reaches of the outfield demanded a Herculean effort seldom repeated. Over time, the distance was condensed to a more reasonable 400 feet, but that didn't necessarily make swinging for the fences a productive habit. Frequent gusts, swirling in from Lake Erie, kept many home run balls inside the park and pushed countless others out of play.

Once in a while, at least during the first 15 years the Indians used Cleveland Stadium, they would return to the more intimate surroundings of League Park. After realizing that operating costs of the larger complex dwarfed that of a 20,000 seat venue, Alva Bradley moved the team completely out of the Stadium in 1934. For three successive seasons, while the team continued its struggle to maintain a large enough following from game to game, the old ball park hosted every home game, while the Stadium sometimes served as a location for the various special events its original boosters had claimed would stimulate the area's economy.

With their team in another clubhouse day in and day out, the public soon began voicing their concern that the city's hard earned dollars had been wasted on nothing more than an expensive monument. Finding himself in no position to alienate more of the team's fans, Bradley decided to use the facility on special occasions. At first, that meant strictly "event" games, such as those played on holidays or weekends, or when attendance was likely to exceed League Park's capacity. But he was still reluctant to pull the Tribe completely out of the hitter's park, since the team's batting statistics benefited from the shorter fences. This way, Bradley could at least make the club seem more exciting than it was.

The shared stadium system ended when Bill Veeck, in his first complete year of ownership, moved his team out of League Park for good at the start of the 1947 season. Four years later, the city bought out the Indians' lease, and converted their original home into a playground.

One of the main reasons League Park became extinct was that it was never furnished with lights. Night baseball had become a way for the 9-5 workday fans and school children to take in a stadium game during the week. Convinced that prime time affairs would bolster yearly attendance, in return creating a greater cash flow, lights were installed on the roof of Cleveland Stadium in 1939.

The original cost to build the Stadium was $3,035,245. In comparison, following 60-some years of inflation, the tab on Jacobs Field rung up at over $200 million. Anyone who has visited Jacobs Field would agree that every cent was spent toward making it one of the Major League's premiere facilities, a place where a day at the ball park becomes a memorable experience. Other baseball teams, hoping to build their own dream stadiums, often name the Indians' home, along with Baltimore's Camden Yards, as inspiration for their desire. With dimensions of 325 feet down the foul lines, and 405 to dead center, the field was designed with the hitter in mind. One of the main features of Jacobs Field is the largest scoreboard in the majors. Perched atop the left field bleachers, and complete with a Sony Jumbotron for instant replays, it is 120 feet high and 220 feet wide.

The conceptualization of Jacobs Field wasn't as easy as merely setting it up on the drawing board and creating a design everyone liked. The finished product would come about after nearly three decades, as denouncements from political factions, businessmen, the owners, and taxpayers defeated several viable proposals for a new facility. Through it all, the threat of the Indians moving out of the city loomed large in the public's conscience, popping up like a migraine headache every time discussions of leaving Cleveland Stadium commenced.

Talks began as early as the mid-1960s, but the first proposal to proceed beyond the planning stages was a 1984 effort to finance a domed stadium in the downtown area. With a projected capacity of 72,000 and a $150 million price tag, the facility was supposed to be the home of Cleveland's three major sports franchises, the Indians, the NFL Browns and the NBA Cavaliers. One major snag prevented the idea from becoming a reality. Money needed for the completion of the project would have been raised by increasing property taxes over the next 25 years. County voters overwhelmingly rejected the resolution.

Part of the problem with playing in Cleveland Stadium was that Browns owner Art Modell, as president of a group known as the Cleveland Stadium Corporation, gained control of the lease in 1974. Dissatisfied with their role as Modell's tenants, and tired of bickering with his company about the escalating costs of their rental agreement, the baseball team filed a lawsuit against Stadium Corporation in 1983. Modell retaliated by suing the Indians. If they fought like cats and dogs during this period, the Indians resembled a wannabe stray meowing and scratching at the door, while Modell assumed the position of a pit bull guarding the steps outside. Before matters worsened, a deal was made out of court, but the relationship between the two organizations had decayed beyond the point of repair.

So, knowing the history between the Indians and Modell, in hindsight, it would seem that sharing a dome would have only intensified their disputes. Since the facility had been Modell's labor of love for some time, adding his penchant for wielding a knife large enough to stab the back of an entire city, together with his eager sense of business, in the long run a joint stadium would have proved to be a very limited partnership for the other parties involved. Though such evidence wasn't apparent at the time, nor was team leverage a direct factor in the public's decision, the voters knew what they were doing.

Time Out:
I know what some of you are thinking. If the stadium had been built, Cleveland would have never lost the Browns. Actually, who knows what Modell would have done if he got his way. His actions showed everyone that he couldn't be trusted. He probably would have driven the Indians

and the Cavaliers away, and *still* moved his football team to Baltimore.

Time In:
   Other, less enthusiastic efforts were made. One called for another dome, which would be dubbed the Hexatron, due to its odd six-sided architecture. Once again, it would have been a home by committee, but the proposal never found its way onto a ballot. Also never materializing was an idea for a dome, complete with a retractable roof similar to Toronto's Sky Dome. The overall cost, thought to be equal to the $400 million dollar price of the Toronto complex, killed the plan immediately.
   If anything, the Tribe's failed attempts to find a new residence delivered a message to Cleveland sports fans. It seemed more evident than ever that the team would wander from the Stadium. The only question was how far away would they go?
   Both the Indians ownership and the offices of Major League Baseball made it clear to the city that the only way for their team to remain was to build a new stadium. Today it's a story we read often in the sports pages, particularly when it comes to baseball and football organizations demanding a new facility. Fortunately for Cleveland, they managed to hold onto a dear friend, if only by a whisker.
   A key turning point in the Tribe's search for a life outside Cleveland Stadium came in 1986, when the Jacobs brothers, Richard and David, bought the club in mid-season. Their ideal place was an open air ball park with a grass surface. The area chosen was a site bordered by three streets in the southern quarters of downtown: East 9th Street, Carnegie Avenue, and Ontario Street. At around 42,800 seats, the new owners vowed it would be used for Indians games only. A neighboring arena used mostly by the Cavaliers, but also featuring other indoor events, eventually became part of the plan.
   In order for the plan to work—and for the city to keep the Indians—community leaders who favored the proposal had to convince the numerous businesses and political entities, as well as the citizens, whose involvement would be necessary for financial approval, that the Gateway Sports and Entertainment Complex was a good, even prosperous idea for the apex of downtown Cleveland. They promised that the new facilities would bring excess customers to restaurants, hotels, shops, and

the various entertainment venues that existed there. The ball park and the adjacent arena would also serve as monuments to the area's new renovation movement.

Under an agreement reached by city officials and the owners of the Indians and Cavaliers, half the sum of the construction costs would be paid by the teams and private investments, while the rest was subject to public funding. Of course, the dilemma was finding a resolution tax payers would vote in favor of. The resolution of choice was a "sin tax". What's a "sin tax", you may be asking? Is the Lord Almighty keeping a running tab on all the times we break a commandment? If so, before we die, we all better hope to inherit a million dollars that are negotiable in the afterlife. No, in this case, a "sin tax" was added to all sales of alcohol and cigarettes in Cuyahoga County. Once the bill passed through state legislation, it was up to voters to decide the fate of the Indians.

On May 8, 1990, over 380,000 citizens voted on the issue. After the ballots were tallied, the city of Cleveland still had its baseball team and the Indians would soon have a ball park of their own. Approval rating on the "sin tax" was a slim 1.2 percent, but it was enough for the project to get officially under way the following month.

By now, it is apparent to everyone who knows the Indians that the new ball park was named after Dick Jacobs. Some fans don't realize that it wasn't necessarily an obligatory honor. Mr. Jacobs paid a fee of $13.9 million for the naming rights for a 20-year period. The original lease signed by Jacobs was also for 20 years.

President Bill Clinton was an Indians fan during the first game ever played in Jacobs Field. He threw out the inaugural first pitch, tossing it as if he was more concerned about getting back to his luxury box to eat the Big Mac his chief political consultant, James Carville, had run out to get during the opening ceremonies. The Tribe's opponent that day was the Seattle Mariners. Randy Johnson took the mound for the visitors, hurling a no-hitter through seven innings. At that point, the Mariners led 2-0, and threatened to spoil the city's celebration. But the Indians were a team as revitalized as the fans' love for them. They fought back to take a 4-3 victory in 11 innings to make the occasion complete.

What else could a fan want? The Indians were winning again. Life was good in the new ball park.

It still is. In fact, there's no place like Jacobs Field. Of course, it would only be fair if every tax paying citizen of Cuyahoga County were given a complimentary hot dog with their ticket stub. Or some peanuts at least.

After all, they helped pay for those seats they're sitting in.

JIM HEGAN
CLEVELAND INDIANS

LUKE EASTER
CLEVELAND INDIANS

AL ROSEN
CLEVELAND INDIANS

RAY BOONE
CLEVELAND INDIANS

5
Fortune's Trick Pitch

It should not take a tragic accident for a baseball player to grab the headlines. How ironic that Fortune would wind up with Expectation in the batter's box and deliver a trick pitch, one that travels with remarkable velocity, then tails up and in at the last, fleeting instant. Gone is the chance to send that ball sailing over the wall for a moment of exaltation. Gone are the opportunities at achieving glory or fulfilling a life long dream.

Destiny is an uncaring foe. It will take away a player's career at the drop of a cap. And Destiny doesn't mind if it strikes on or off the field. What's saddest in some cases is that tragedy becomes a stepping stone for an obscure player's 15 minutes of fame.

Cliff Young was a name most of us had never heard of. On the morning of November 5, 1993, the nation's newspapers introduced us to him, but we couldn't make a mental note of an up-and-coming player that we could root for come spring training. We could only honor his memory with a moment of silence.

Young pitched in only 21 games, seven of which were starts, during his shortened career with Cleveland. He won three of those games and lost just as many. Though his statistics might not have been evidence of a sprouting legend, time simply didn't allow his ability to see the light of day. Signed by the team the previous winter, he had spent the majority of his career in the minors. He appeared in 28 games with California in 1990 and '91.

His life was brought to a premature end when the car he was driving spun off the road and smashed into a tree. Accounts of the accident later revealed that Young was attempting to light a cigarette when he lost control of the vehicle.

Fortune glanced at him for a brief moment. Then it brought the ball to it's glove, kicked up a leg, and threw a curve ball.

That incident was not the first disaster to befall the Indians. It was not even the first tragedy that year.

March 22, 1993. Even now it rings with a quiver in the voice, a tightening of the throat. On that day, the Cleveland Indians and the world of baseball, as well as all of humanity, found out life can be carefree one moment and incredibly unsympathetic the next.

It was a day like any other day for America. We awoke, had our coffee and breakfast, and drove to work or set out to begin the tasks of a spring morning that would result in an ordinary semblance of life. We performed our daily duties with an air of indifference to the one thing that can take the happiness out of our routine. Nobody counts on tragedy striking at any given moment, but for the Cleveland Indians and the families of three of the team's players, March 22 was a day that the world stopped.

For Tim Crews, an off-season acquisition formerly with the Los Angeles Dodgers, the start of the new day held a small promise that it would be different from the tedium of a ball player's life during spring training. It was the only break the Indians had in their exhibition schedule. So, like the other players on the team, his thoughts turned to family and fun.

He invited some of his new teammates and their families to his ranch on Little Lake Nellie near Clermont, Florida, just 27 miles from the Indians training site in Winter Haven. Two of the players who joined him were fellow pitchers Bob Ojeda and Steve Olin. They spent the entire day there, picnicking and taking their children horse back riding. There were no worries that day. Just fun. Relaxing in the Florida sun and getting to know one another for the long season ahead. As close to a perfect day as a ball player could have without winning a game.

So they made the best of it, extracting as much good time out of the remaining hours as they could. By nightfall, the three pitchers set out on the small lake in Crews's 18-foot, motorized fishing boat. Settled out on the lake for only a few minutes, they saw a set of headlights flashing in the distance. That was a signal. There were more passengers who just arrived on shore. Such a horrible twist of fate that a pitcher's last signal didn't come from a catcher, or a coach standing in the dugout, or that it wasn't a fat pitch taken out of the park in a crucial situation that brought an abrupt end to his career. Tim Crews didn't bother to shake off this signal. He wasn't thinking about home runs, or baseball for that matter, when he revved the engine of his boat and headed for the banks of Little Lake Nellie at 39 mph beneath the veil of a southern night sky.

He guided the boat into a wide turn in order to navigate toward the area where the now unlit car was parked. Only a few feet away was a dock that extended some 250 feet out into the lake. Without a light nearby, it was more of an extension of the night to their eyes. The boat veered head on into the dock. The three players, sitting upright, next to one another, took the majority of the impact from the chest up.

It happened in the amount of time it takes to split an atom. Lives were lost. Others, those of the player's loved ones, were changed forever. The Indians' season became one of mourning.

Crews died in a hospital a few hours after the accident, due to a massive head injury. He was 31. Surviving him were a wife and three children.

Bob Ojeda, the only player to survive the accident, was the most widely known of the three. He was a member of the World Champion New York Mets in 1986, his most productive year in the majors. He posted an 18-5 record and a 2.57 ERA during that campaign. With Cleveland, he was expected to have a significant role in the starting rotation. That changed the moment the boat collided with the dock. He severed the top of his skull in the accident, resulting in a near death from loss of blood.

Somehow, he managed to make a comeback on August 7, of that season. He made seven starts for the Indians the rest of the way, winning twice and losing once. The following year, he signed a free agent contract with the Yankees. After two starts, in which he struggled to find his control, and with his life turned on it's side by the incident on Little Lake Nellie, Ojeda left the game of baseball.

That he was able to comeback at all is a testament to his personal fortitude. Not only did he have his own physical injuries to overcome, he was involved in an enduring battle against the psychological trauma that haunted him. He underwent months of rehabilitation, plastic surgery, and counseling. For Bob Ojeda, the memory of that night may drift from time to time, but it never fades away.

Crews and Ojeda were veterans looking forward to a new opportunity in a new city on a new team. Who knows? Maybe their careers would have been born again in Cleveland. But Fortune picked them off with the thoughtlessness of plucking apples off a tree.

Maybe Steve Olin was reaching his prime. After showing he was equal to the task the previous season, he was expected to be the team's dominant closer. In '92, he saved 29 games and posted a scant 2.34 earned run average. Drafted in the 16th round in 1987, he was a product of the Indians' farm system. With a young, lively arm, and a major role on an up-and-coming team, there was nothing but great expectations for him.

Death came instantly. Took him off the face of the earth without a second of contemplation. Like Crews, Olin left behind a wife and three children.

All the sacrifices suffered through. The long, uncompromising hours of practice, dedication, sore arms, those cold moments of doubt late at night questioning if it was worth it, if he was good enough to be in the majors; traveling to different cities, different ball parks, day in and day out, night after night. And then to have Fortune turn on him and take it away at the very moment it all seemed to be paying off.

Maybe Steve Olin would be a star reliever. Maybe he would be a hero, striking out the final batter in the World Series.

We will never know.

The Indians have had a long history of tragedy. Fortune's wild streak began as early as 1910, inflicting it's harm on one of the team's greatest pitchers of all time.

Calling him a pitcher would be shortchanging Addie Joss. He was a legend. A record of 160 wins and only 97 defeats over eight-plus seasons attests to that. More striking was his 1.89 career ERA. Come to think of it, Legend doesn't even begin to serve his memory well enough.

If you were able to watch newsreel footage of him, or were lucky enough to have seen him pitch, the only justifiable description of Joss would be that he was an artist. He was a thinking man's pitcher who could blow a fastball by the most guarded hitter. Trying to catch a piece of his curve was like trying to take a fish out of water with your bare hand. Control was his middle name, as evidenced by a career ratio of 1.43 walks per nine innings. Many referred to his exaggerated delivery as a pinwheel motion, but his pitches were often like brush strokes that gave life to some new masterpiece. For instance, his first major league appearance on April 26, 1902 was the greatest pitching debut in the history of the game. All the St. Louis Browns could muster that day was one hit. *One!* And the validity of that hit was debatable. It came on a sinking line drive off the bat of Jesse Burkett. Indians rightfielder Elmer Flick claimed he scooped the ball into his glove and saved it from touching the ground. Originally, the play was called an out, but umpire Bill Carruthers said Flick trapped it and overruled the decision. Cleveland won the game, 3-0, and Joss began his journey toward baseball immortality. Along with five career one-hitters and one no-hitter, he tossed a perfect game on October 2, 1908. Historians still call Joss's clutch performance against the Chicago White Sox on that blustery day one of the finest exhibitions of pitching power and wit ever displayed. One stat that would sky rocket his value on today's market is his 234 complete games in 286 starts. If a team had an entire rotation equal to Joss's talent, their relief pitchers would be milling around stick ball games hoping to find work.

A sore arm in 1910 limited him to only 13 games and a 5-5 record. During a comeback bid the following spring, it became obvious that something was wrong. He lost a considerable amount of weight. At the end of March, during an exhibition game in Chattanooga, Tennessee he fainted on the dugout bench. Before the start of the season, chest pains and a consistently high fever prompted doctors to recommend him to return home to Toledo. His condition, known as pleurisy, worsened over the next few days.

On April 14, 1911, Joss passed away at the tragically young age of 31. Cause of death was tubercular meningitis. Surviving him was a wife of nine years, a son, and a daughter.

The Indians' season opener was delayed so that teammates and adoring fans could attend funeral services and pay homage to his memory. He was admired so much by the people he played for and against that the American League organized a charity game in which all proceeds were donated to his family. That says a lot as to what kind of ball player Joss was. It says a great deal more about what kind of a human being he was.

Fortune does not care who it turns on.

On August 16, 1920, Indians shortstop Ray Chapman stepped up to the plate at the Polo Grounds to face Fortune in the form of New York Yankees pitcher Carl Mays. It was the fifth inning of a meaningful game. Both clubs were entangled in the pennant race, along with the defending AL champion Chicago White Sox. Going into the game, Cleveland held a game and a half lead over New York, and a two-game edge over the ChiSox. Chapman led off the fifth inning with his team ahead, 3-0, on a damp, slightly sloppy field.

Chapman had a joking, easy going personality that could liven up the dullest room. On train trips to road games, it was usually Chapman who inspired his teammates to join in on a song to alleviate the tension and boredom of a long journey. Although he was 29 years old, he had the face of a boy whose ears stuck out beneath the rim of his cap. It was a genuine face. One with a cheery outlook, and his smile, his lighthearted temperament, even when morale was at a low point, were a welcome relief on the Indians bench. His wife Kathleen was back home in Cleveland while the game was being played.

Carl Mays had the reputation of a bean ball artist. Two years before, he hit Indian great Tris Speaker in the head with an errant pitch. Prior incidents of head-hunting were taken into account and many believed that the tactic was part of his repertoire. Another accusation aimed at Mays over his career was that he deliberately scuffed baseballs. A nicked ball would produce a more erratic delivery. In defense of Mays, the way he threw a ball had a lot to do with that stigma. Due to his twisting body and low, submarine-style delivery, the ball would sometimes take off unexpectedly, making catcher the hardest fielding position on the diamond.

Back in 1920, batters didn't wear protective helmets. The only thing protecting their skull from the ball was a very thin layer of skin and flesh and the pitcher's aim.

Chapman crouched down in his usual stance, crowding the right side of the plate. As Mays's pitch twisted a little high and a little to the inside, he froze. Eye witnesses of the incident claimed to have heard an explosive crack. The ball rolled toward the pitcher's mound, where Mays, believing it hit the bat, tossed it to first. Wally Pipp stepped on the bag, then pivoted to throw the ball around the infield when he caught a glimpse of Chapman slumped to the ground near home plate.

Players from both teams surrounded him, while physicians placed ice compresses to the head wound. Blood streamed from the player's left ear, but he maintained consciousness long enough to sit up. With the assistance of teammates, Chapman struggled to his feet. He refused further help and began walking, staggering toward the center field clubhouse. As a precautionary measure, two of his teammates followed close behind. Applause erupted from the stands, but soon muffled as the player wobbled near second base. His teammates held him up, placing his arms behind their necks. Relieved, fans and fellow ball players cheered once more as he was carried off the field, believing his consciousness to be a sign that the injury was not threateningly serious.

After being told about the circumstances, a panic-stricken Kathleen Chapman took an overnight train to New York, arriving the next morning. Her husband had gone into surgery shortly after midnight that same morning. His skull had suffered a three inch fracture on the left side. Impact from the blow had also shifted his brain to the right side, causing a massive concussion. Surgeons removed a 1 ½ inch piece of skull that had lodged in his brain and initiated a rupture.

Kathleen was summoned to the team hotel. A room full of players, including manager-centerfielder Tris Speaker, were waiting in silence. Their faces, the choked back sobs evident in their eyes, told her what she had dreaded and prayed against during the passing of a lonely night on a long train ride.

Her husband was dead. Chapman lapsed into unconsciousness prior to the operation and never woke up. Time of death was determined to be at 4:35 on Tuesday morning, August 17.

All of Cleveland fell silent that day. It was as if the sky had closed it's eyes and cast a shadow of sorrow over families' kitchens, over the entire business community, and school yards, a sorrow that found its way down every alley, into every corner of every building, and made work and the day's duties seem all the less important. Ray Chapman was dead! People on the sidewalks read the morning editions with a vacant, somber gaze in their eyes.

The game scheduled for the Polo Grounds that afternoon was canceled. To the Baseball community and a nation of fans, the death of Ray Chapman had the impact of a brutal slaying in a small, close-knit town. *It couldn't happen here.*

But it did. And Major League Baseball, the city of Cleveland, and its beloved Indians had to deal with it and move on through the re-mainder of a marred season. Kathleen Chapman had to cope with the emptiness of a new world.

Carl Mays had to live with the incident for the rest of his life as well. Immediately following his death, a faction of Chapman's teammates said they believed the pitch was intentional. The Yankee pitcher claimed it was an accident. Speaker quickly put out the impending fire by personally stating he didn't hold Mays responsible, admitting that the occurrence of such a freak accident could be blamed solely on chance taking a turn for the worse. It was a dark hour for a game that revolved around chance, and his team would honor their friend's memory and uphold Baseball's reputation by displaying an indomitable spirit. They would focus on winning games and not accusing a fellow ball player of deliberate injury.

That's not to say Speaker didn't feel the loss. Stricken so much by grief, he was unable to attend the funeral held in St. John's Cathedral in Cleveland.

Still, there were some who weren't easily persuaded into dropping their charges against Mays. Other teams who had been susceptible to his lack of control, began talks of boycotting any games in which Mays took part. It's easy to understand their point. Baseball, like any sport, is a game of emotions. Fortunately, for the good of the Game, nothing came of the threat, and the 1920 season went on to become memorable in other aspects. Certainly for the Indians, who paid tribute to their fallen teammate by winning the World Series over the Brooklyn Robins.

A slick fielder, Chapman also knew what to do with the bat. He possessed good speed, which often put the hurt on catchers around the league once he reached base. He joined the Indians in 1912, and compiled a .278 lifetime batting average while swiping 233 bases. In 1917, he stole 52, a number that stood as a franchise record until 1980. His leadership and pep talks held the infield together.

It has often been speculated that Ray Chapman was on his way to the Hall of Fame. All he needed was time.

Fortune doesn't wear a wrist watch. Nor does it plan at what moment it will get a fateful break on one of its pitches.

A twi-night doubleheader was scheduled for July 10, 1947, in Cleveland Stadium against the Philadelphia Athletics. On the mound for the Indians during the first game was Don Black, a man who had a lot to prove to his team and all those who gave him a second and third chance at a career in Baseball.

He had been battling misfortune for some time. Originally with the Athletics for three seasons, Black was suspended from the organization in 1945 due to excessive drinking. The Indians purchased his contract on October 2 of that year. The next season he struggled with his new team, posting an ERA above 4.50 and managing one win and two defeats in 18 appearances. Again, drinking became a deterrent, forcing Indians owner Bill Veeck to order his pitcher to join Alcoholics Anonymous. During this period, it was uncertain whether or not he would ever pitch in the big leagues again, much less for the Tribe.

A successful rehab gave him a new order in life. It allowed him to remain with Cleveland, and he pitched impressively, making 28 starts in 1947. 10 of the outings resulted in victories, while 12 were losses, but his ERA dropped by over half a point from the previous season. One evening in particular his mastery of the opposition assured that his name would be forever included in the record books.

Facing his old team during the first game of the doubleheader was not a cause for revenge for Black. He knew it was his own undoing that severed the ties between him and the Athletics. The Indians were falling in the standings, and he wanted to do whatever was in his power to win. It must have been magical powers that he possessed that day. Allowing six walks and striking out five is a mediocre outing at best, but not giving up a single hit was a milestone achieved by only eight other Tribe pitchers up to that time.

The new found success was short-lived. In 1948, he made occasional starts for an Indians team that was involved in a heated pennant race with three other club. On September 13, manager Lou Boudreau called on Black for one of those spot starts. In the second inning of the game versus the St. Louis Browns at home, he fouled off a pitch on a wild swing. After the follow through, he stumbled, then walked behind the home plate umpire. A moment later, he slumped to the ground, unconscious, the result of a brain hemorrhage.

Doctors figured he had a fifty-fifty chance for survival. He was in critical condition for more than a week before slowly recovering. For a month, he remained in a hospital bed, until he was able to resume a normal life.

Except, it was a life without baseball. He never threw another pitch, or swung another bat in the Major Leagues. After battling back from the depths of alcohol abuse, it seemed as if his career had steadied. Then Fortune's trick pitch caught him off guard.

Nothing but greatness loomed on the horizon for Herb Score. Facing him, most batters were under the impression that his left arm was a launching pad for missiles. As a rookie in 1955, he fanned 245 of his opponents (an AL rookie record) en route to winning 16 out of 26 decisions. After that, he became simply awesome. A 20-9 record in 1956 included an earned run average of 2.53 and a league leading 263 K's. With numbers like that, a blazing fastball, and the hopes of the Indians future riding on his prized left arm, many viewed him as the reflective image of the greatest pitcher the Indians ever had, Bob Feller, who retired in '56, after passing the torch to Score.

Score was a perfectionist, a habit that drove him to improve any faults he may have had. After a day's performance he'd pick apart his mistakes. It didn't matter if it was a victory. He'd try to figure out how to perfect them for his next start. He worked hard, even during practice.

It was this combination of healthy attitude and incomparable talent that led Tom Yawkey, owner of the Boston Red Sox, to pitch $1 million at the Indians in an effort to obtain the youngster in 1957. The Indians flat out refused and quipped that they wouldn't even consider it for double the amount. Back then, entire franchises cost less than the top free agents make today. A million dollars exchanged for one player was considered extravagant.

But you can't put a price tag on unlimited talent. Then again, you can't count on Fortune playing by the rules, either.

Many baseball experts and fans who saw him pitch believe Herb Score would have become the most dominant lefty the game has ever known. They compare the potential he displayed to the mound prowess of Sandy Koufax, who won three Cy Young awards and threw four no-hitters during his career with the Brooklyn-Los Angeles Dodgers from 1955-66. Of course, its all speculation now.

The Indians played the Yankees at the Stadium on May 7, 1957. It was Score's fifth start of the year. Hank Bauer grounded out to Tribe third baseman Al Smith to lead off the game. The Yankees' second batter, Gil McDougald, who could knock the seams off a ball, worked Score to a two and two count before Fortune stepped in to alter history for the worse.

Score fired low and away.

After the game, McDougald would say he didn't know how he got his bat on the ball, but he did. He managed to get the fat of the wood on it and sent a rocket line drive up the middle. Since the momentum of his follow through brought Score off the mound, rendering him defenseless at the moment of contact, he had less than a split second to react. He couldn't get his glove up in time to act as a shield. The ball smacked his right cheek bone with the fury of a rifle blast, and knocked him to the ground.

With Score reeling in agony, blood covering half his face, McDougald froze midway down the first base line. The ball careened toward third where Smith picked it up, and hesitated, looking toward his fallen teammate. He recovered from shock long enough to throw McDougald out, then ran over to the pitcher.

Score never lost consciousness. Throughout the ordeal, he remained at ease. While waiting for an ambulance in the clubhouse, he joked that his face looked as bad as a fighter who had gone 10 rounds. Though he couldn't see out of his right eye, doctors at the Lakeside Hospital assured him he would regain his vision. He remained in the hospital for three weeks, the first of which was spent in total darkness.

McDougald knew he had no control over where the ball would go once it leapt off his bat, but he suffered nonetheless from the traumatic effects of seeing a ball he hit nearly take off the head of another player. All memories of that day for him were confined to the image of Score's head snapping back, blood spurting on impact. It haunted him through-out the remainder of his career. Nobody blames him. Yet, his name is forever attached to the hit that nearly blinded the Indians southpaw.

The rest of the '57 season was lost for Score. Many Indians followers feared that his pitching days were over as well. To this day, there are those who believe the eye injury ruined his career.

That's not entirely true. It would have been easy for him to shy away from the pitching mound after such a scary incident, but Score was as competitive as they come. He made a valiant comeback the following year, starting the season opener. The Tribe lost to the Kansas City Athletics that day, by a score of 5-0, but by the time of his third start, he was as overpowering as when he was a rookie. He struck out 13 White Sox hitters en route to a shutout. With his comeback bid a success, he turned his attention toward reclaiming the greatness he rightly deserved.

Just at the moment it seemed he had overcome adversity and turned Fortune around, back in his favor, bad luck struck again. During a night game in Washington, he tore a tendon in his throwing elbow. With a tender arm, he lost some zip on his pitches, and his control wasn't what it used to be. Knowing he wouldn't be effective with a lame duck fastball, Score retired from the game in 1962, after being traded and serving a two-year stint with the White Sox.

His competitive nature was so strong that he was able to elude Fortune's initial curve ball. The Indians and their legion of fans could only regret, for one heckuva long time, that Fortune has more than one trick pitch in its arsenal. Herb Score was going to be the soul of a winning team. Everything seemed to change with one vicious crack of a bat.

More tribulations followed.

An up-and-coming outfielder by the name of Walter Bond was diagnosed with leukemia in the early '60s. He died in 1967, only 29 years old.

Max Alvis, a player many hoped would help Cleveland establish another golden age, reminiscent of the Tribe teams of the early '50s, was bedridden with spinal meningitis in 1964. Though he courageously continued playing and became one of the most inspirational players in team history, he never fully reached his potential.

In 1966, shortstop Larry Brown and left fielder Leon Wagner ran into one another while converging on a shallow fly ball. Brown suffered multiple skull fractures and lapsed into a coma for three days. A week later he was released from the hospital and was able to resume his playing career later in the season. He never put up great numbers, but remained a good fielder for five more seasons.

With their string of hazards continuing into the '70s, it would be reasonable to believe that the Indians had fallen victim to a curse at some time or another during their long history. Maybe there was a witch doctor roaming the streets of Cleveland, sticking pins into dolls with baseball caps. Maybe there just aren't enough Tribe fans in the afterlife. Guardian angels probably root for the Anaheim ball club.

Either way, it was just the Indians luck that one of their most promising young players was involved in one of the most memorable plays ever, one we still see on highlight reels from time to time. Of course, I'm talking about Pete Rose crashing into Tribe catcher Ray Fosse to win the 1970 All-Star game for the National League. On the play, Fosse suffered a serious injury to his left shoulder that hampered him the rest of his career. He never regained the authority of a once productive swing.

Another promising prospect on the Indians roster that year was Tony Horton. A 27-home run season in 1969 gave the organization a glimpse of the power the young man possessed. It also gave him leverage to hold out the following spring while trying to renegotiate his contract for a $5,000 raise. The team refused to increase his salary. Still, once he rejoined the club before the start of the season, his image was tarnished in the eyes of the everyday fan. Making matters worse, manager Alvin Dark continuously fed the media comments about Horton's sub-par ability at first base. Determined to prove Dark wrong and excel at the plate as well, he drove himself to emotional exhaustion.

After failing to get a hit in two plate appearances during the second game of a doubleheader against the Angels on August 28, 1970, Dark yanked him from the lineup. Fuming, Horton immediately left the dugout and went into the clubhouse where he suffered a nervous breakdown. He attempted suicide and was hospitalized for a short time. After recovering, he never played the game again.

Horton ended his career as an Indian with 76 homers in nearly four seasons and left behind a player's most feared legacy. People who remember Tony Horton always end up asking the same question. What if?

While Horton was holding out, the man the organization had traded for to take over at first base broke his right ankle during an exhibition game in March. Never fully healing from the injury, Ken Harrelson failed to make the kind of impact on the club fans, teammates, and the front office presumed he would. Most of all, they hoped he would bolster offensive production and increase home attendance. With the Boston Red Sox in 1969, he clubbed 35 round-trippers and batted in a league high 109 runs, earning AL Player of the Year honors. So, the Indians had one of the top power-hitters of the day. For a total of 67 games, that is. He made a comeback late in the '70 season, and nearly played the first third of the following year before retiring for good.

I guess all that can be said of the Ken Harrelson trade is that it was one of those sure-shot gambles that misfired. Blame Fortune for it's ineptitude.

Without question, one of the most consistent power-hitters in Tribe history was Andre Thornton. He blasted a total of 253 home runs during his nine-plus season career with Cleveland. If not for two knee operations, a dislocated shoulder, and other various injuries, as well as a lack of hitting talent around him, Thornton could have left the game holding a one-way ticket to Cooperstown.

Fortune cheated the Indians a little, the same way it did several times before. Yet, because Thornton had an unbeatable will, they still had a great player.

Andre was not as lucky. He was cheated much worse by Fortune, suffering a personal loss that could easily have wiped out any man's desire to go on with an everyday living, much less to play the Game and still succeed admirably at it.

He came to Cleveland via a trade with the Montreal Expos in the winter prior to the 1977 season. In his first year with the Tribe, he hit 28 homers, collected 70 RBIs, and scored an additional 77 runs. It was a perfect version of the American dream, one with a prosperous career, and most importantly, a loving family. He had a wife, Gertrude, a son named Andy and daughter named Theresa. Their future together appeared to be bright. There were no warning signs of despair on the horizon.

But that's when tragedy reaches in and hits the hardest.

Thornton and his family were driving home to attend a wedding in West Chester, Pennsylvania at the tail end of his first year with the

Indians. They were traveling in the family van. Andre was driving. Some time during the trip, the winter weather acted up. A violent gust of wind caught the van and pushed it off the turnpike. Andre and his son survived the accident, but his wife and daughter weren't as lucky.

He was no different than anyone before or after who has suffered from personal anguish. He struggled to face the agony and searched for answers like the rest of us would. But his experience is one of triumph for the human spirit. It is an uplifting story of a man's mental and physical strength, of his ability to believe.

Where did he find the solace and the comfort needed in such a time of mourning? He went to church. He read the bible. He prayed to God and listened to His word.

Thornton also wrote a book about dealing with his painful experience. The title of the book is *Triumph Born of Tragedy*. In it, he explains first hand that, through devotion in God, we are given the strength to go on.

That is a saving grace not even Fortune can take away with a trick pitch.

6
<u>So Close,</u>
<u>So Far Away</u>

Expectations are born and raised, but hopes are meant to be shot down and burned to the ground.

And in Cleveland, they're always waiting for a Phoenix to rise out of the ashes and reach the heights of glory. Instead, they're usually left shaking their heads, echoing the sentiment that it'll be a long time coming after all.

Yes, that is a negative mindset, but you can't blame Indians fans for being pessimistic come crunch time. Not after waiting over 40 years to reach the promised land, only to come up short. Especially after believing one too many times that *this is the year*! No. Something will go wrong. So you tell yourself. Remember, these are the Indians. Not the Yankees.

These are heaven's version of a sense of humor. A bad one at that. At times, they've been the Bad News Bears grown up. Or the un-attractive bridesmaid who never makes it to the altar.

The same old, same old.

I don't know. Is there satisfaction in going to a dance with your dream date, only to have the DJ forget to play a slow song? Is there any satisfaction in going to Florida in the middle of winter, only to have it rain every day you're there? How about getting to game six of the World Series, then having your hot bats freeze up in the autumn winds. Is there any *real* satisfaction?

Is the heartbreak less painful when the Indians have the best record in Baseball, only to crumble to a wild-card in the playoffs? At least when they died peacefully in mid-July, everyone was over it in time for football season.

There is a stronger force tugging at the heart when your team reaches the post-season. Unfortunately, the Indians of the mid-'90s have yet to bring home a World Series title. They've been as close as late October, yet as far away as next season.

But, along the way you realize what a wonderful journey it is.

It must have been the uncanny fan support, right? Or the aura of playing in a brand new ball park? Or the patience of an organization intent on rebuilding during the early stages of the decade? And what about all the key acquisitions in the previous off-seasons?

Try all four. It takes a whole lotta shakin' to build a winner out of a perennial loser.

If anything, the 1994 season will be remembered as the year Baseball's most hapless franchise for four decades running transformed into a contender. It may not have been evident at the time, but the process of turning the franchise around was in full swing during the team's worst season ever. In 1991, the Tribe lost 105 games, and by then, fans had the impression that their ball club would never give them reason to cheer. Of course, a team does not get that bad by accident.

The front office men decided to bare the skeleton. Their '91 version of a baseball team consisted of minor leaguers, low-cost rent-a-vets, and young players with potential who also came at a cheap price. In the baseball vernacular, these Indians were a bunch of nobodies. Some of them would only be for a short time. Most of the veteran talent they did have was shipped out to other teams for handfuls of prospects, or otherwise let go. By '92, high-priced pitchers, Greg Swindell, Tom Candiotti, and Doug Jones were gone. Other moves were made to reduce the pay roll, as well.

It made sense. Why keep a more costly team that would finish in the middle of the standings anyway? Why not rebuild the farm system and look to a bright future? It was a plan that worked only because management, by sacrificing their highest paid players, was saving a pool of money that would be used to secure the young talent they were accumulating.

They said so long to Joe Carter, and hello to Sandy Alomar, Jr., and Carlos Baerga after completing a deal with the San Diego Padres before the 1990 season. Two years later, Kenny Lofton was acquired from the Houston Astros for catcher Eddie Taubensee. Another prize acquisition, who became as instrumental to the team's success as any other player, was closer Jose Mesa. Cleveland scouts liked what they saw in his lively arm. They just didn't know if he had the ability to control his fastball. Neither did the Baltimore Oriole brain trust. So the Tribe stole him for the price of a minor leaguer on July 14, 1992.

Also key to their building process was the organization's knack for drafting wisely. Joey Belle and Charles Nagy were high selections in 1988 and '89 respectively. Joey later changed his name to Albert, and when he was not firing baseballs at fans or swearing at the media, he was using his stick to launch bombs into the upper decks. Jim Thome followed as a 13th round choice in '89. Usually, he hit about half as many homers as Belle (still an impressive amount), but spectators didn't need to wear protective armor when he held the ball. Manny Ramirez, who has as much corkless clout in the barrel of his bat as anyone, was drafted in the first round of the '91 June draft. Pitcher Chad Ogea was a third round selection that year.

So, by 1994, the Cleveland Indians were ready to challenge the baseball world with their stable of young talent. Well, almost ready. They still needed a few hired hands to ensure success. Dick Jacobs threw his philosophy of penny-pinching out the window. First, the team signed their own top players to lucrative deals, then they shopped the market and found some bargains. Both Eddie Murray and Dennis Martinez joined the Tribe for over $3 million a year. Omar Vizquel came over from the Mariners for $2.3 million a season. It was the best team the Indians fielded in a long time.

Major League Baseball, like the Indians, also completed a transformation in '94. Both leagues switched to a three division format. Formerly a member of the AL East, Cleveland was now located in the newly formed Central Division.

That wasn't the only change. Post-season entrants were increased by two. Instead of two division winners battling each other for the right to represent their respective leagues in the Fall Classic, the new playoff system allowed the top finishers in each division and a wild-card team, the second place team with the best record, to qualify. It was a move similar to the one the NFL made in 1970 when rules were changed to let wild-cards into the post-season. With playoff chances doubled, pennant fever would spread to more parts of the country, and more tickets would sell. That was what baseball hoped for.

It worked.

Fan interest in many cities neared an all-time high, especially in Cleveland, where the Indians were the hottest ticket of summer '94. With Albert Belle's bat—not his ego—coming of age, the Indians had the most feared lineup in the game.

Speaking of Belle, the oft-scrutinized slugger found himself in the middle of a controversy that summer. It came at a time when Tribe fans hoped their team could distance themselves from the Chicago White Sox in the AL Central Division. Cleveland held a half game lead in the standings when the two teams met for a showcase series at Comiskey Park immediately after the All-Star break. Chicago won the first game, 6-3, on the evening of July 14, behind a 12-strikeout performance by Alex Fernandez. During the game, Belle launched a tape measure home run that became the shot that triggered World War III. Or at least a circus, depending on which way you look at it.

Gene Lamont, the Sox manager, marched his team onto the field of battle the next day with a counter offensive in mind. Hit 'em where it hurts most. His strategy was to take the bat out of the hands of their opponents most potent weapon. Literally. During Belle's first plate appearance, Lamont made an appeal to home plate umpire Dave Phillips to check over his bat. Phillips found no signs of tampering, but the bat was confiscated and taken to the umpire's locker room, on suspicion of being corked. Later, it would be sent to American League headquarters in New York for x-rays.

What difference does it make if a bat is regulation wood or corked? For one thing, a corked bat is lighter, allowing for a quicker swing which can increase distance on a fly ball just enough to take a deep out over the fence. But why would Belle, a guy who could just about hoist a piano on his back, need to cheat to crank out home runs? Well, Belle denied the accusations, of course. He claimed that if his bat was corked, he'd be hitting 'em out every time up.

So, how did Lamont deduce that the bat in question was tainted? Certainly someone of Belle's caliber, someone, mind you, who had a sterling record as an ambassador of good will in Major League circles, was being falsely accused. The most incriminating evidence stemmed from a game in Minnesota the year before. Belle broke his bat while swinging at a pitch. A section of the barrel flew into the stands. He moved quickly to get it back, then offered the excuse that he didn't want any fan in a stadium where they heckled him to have a free souvenir at his expense. To support his belief further, Lamont pointed out some game films in which the Tribe slugger hit opposite field dingers with regularity. Too many other times, Lamont claimed, Belle connected for game winning blasts.

Albert had nothing to worry about. He said he didn't do it. The x-rays would show up negative, his bat would be returned, and he'd continue terrorizing AL pitching.

It wasn't that simple.

Exhibit A was under lock and key on a table behind Phillips's clothes in the crew's dressing room. That's where the story turns from mere incident to crime to full blown conspiracy.

Theories have hence been formulated about who broke into the umpire's locker room to steal the accused wood in an attempt to cover up any wrong doing. Sources indicate that even Oliver Stone has put his two cents worth into the matter, claiming he has figured out who the culprits were and just how the thieves perpetrated the crime, but there is no word yet if a motion picture is in the works. All that is definitely known to this day is that the bat was indeed removed from the room, and it was an internal operation. Some have claimed it was Indians pitcher

Jason Grimsley, but no true evidence has surfaced.

The most popular theory as to how the abduction occurred, puzzled together by investigators soon after, is that the thief's entrance came by way of the air conditioning duct above the ceiling tiles in the visitors' clubhouse. Supposedly, while the game was in progress, a chair in Cleveland manager Mike Hargrove's office was used as a step ladder to enable the person to slide one of the ceiling panels over. The intruder —we'll call him agent 008, in honor of Belle's uniform number—using the wall as leverage, climbed into the ventilation shaft that joined the two rooms. 008 slunk his way along, found the targeted room, and broke through the ceiling panel. He lowered himself onto a refrigerator, then jumped to the floor. After a frantic search, he located Belle's bat, and replaced it with a similar model used by teammate Paul Sorrento. He returned to the Indians clubhouse. For the time being, the covert operation was a success.

In his haste to avoid capture, 008 left Phillips' clothes scattered on the floor and the ceiling tile removed. Perhaps during subsequent spring trainings, Indians management should cut down on base running drills and provide a course in Burglary 101.

Following the game that night, the umpiring crew retired to their ransacked quarters and immediately contacted stadium security. To Lamont and the White Sox organization, it was obvious what had happened. Their rivals attempted to conceal their guilt. After all, nearly half the season remained, and the teams were locked in a glorious confrontation for the title. They would meet one more time during the season, in Cleveland one week later. Knowing that a suspension for the Tribe's most feared hitter could increase their chances to pull ahead, Sox general manager Ron Schueler was ready to press charges of breaking and entering. He threatened to involve the police, but Major League Baseball's acting commissioner Bud Selig intervened, demanding the Cleveland organization to return the stolen property immediately.

Indians GM, John Hart, said the franchise did not condone such an action, calling it "a misguided sense of loyalty." So the Indians had little choice in the matter. The bat was anonymously returned the following afternoon and handed directly over to Baseball's chief of security.

How could the Tribe retaliate? Well, Hargrove decided to play mind games of his own. Sox reliever Dennis Cook was pitching in the seventh inning of the series finale when the Indians manager requested home plate umpire Tim McClelland to inspect the pitcher's equipment for possible ball tampering. McClelland searched Cook's cap and glove for razor blades, Vaseline, any foreign substance that could mar the ball. Nothing. Yet, Hargrove returned to the dugout, satisfied with the sheer delivery of a simple message: Two can play at that game.

Meanwhile, the bat was shipped to the league offices where it was sawed in half. Sure enough, the barrel was stocked with pieces of cork. Belle was penalized with a seven game suspension. He pleaded that it was a frame-up on the part of the White Sox. While it was in their possession, they tampered with it.

One question still persists to this day. Why did Belle and his team covet the return of that bat enough to send one of their own players across enemy lines to retrieve it, as if it was the Ark of the Covenant?

The weekend series and its obvious maneuvers set the tone for a thrilling pennant race to be. The Indians and Sox split the first showdown two games apiece. During the subsequent matchup at Jacobs Field on July 21-24, Chicago took two of the four games, and held a slight edge in the division. Realizing that time was running out, especially with a possible players' strike looming, the Indians surged in early August. The playoffs seemed to be their destiny.

On the night of August 11, the Tribe had a 66-47 record. It was their best winning percentage that late in the season since 1955. The team led the Majors in home runs with 167. They had a league high batting average of .290. Home attendance was on a pace to shatter the franchise record. More importantly, they trailed the White Sox by only a game and led in the wild-card derby. It was going to be a race to remember. One our children and grandchildren would hear about someday when we took them to the ball park to see a newly faltering crew wearing Indians uniforms. Would they believe us? Or would they question it deep down inside, the way we doubted the stories our fathers or grandfathers told us about the Tribe teams of the late '40s and early '50s?

None of it mattered the next morning. That was when the long feared Major League Baseball work stoppage went into affect. The season, the post-season, and all of Cleveland's hopes were wiped away along with the tears from our eyes. In no other city had the strike devastated so many. It was as if a loved one had slammed the door on our face and left us to wait outside through a bitter winter. My, how hard reconciliation would be.

So, we tucked away our hearts for months and faced the world as hard luck orphans put out too many times to believe in promises anymore. Then, as spring approached, our stomachs grumbled. We craved the hearty banquets the game had offered us for so long. We looked at Mr. Baseball, as if he was our keeper, and we held out our plates and said: "Please, sir, we want some more."

Cleveland may have been the only town in the whole country where fans were so willing to forgive. How could anyone blame them? To be so close to triumph, only to have it taken away by shrewd politics, greed, and stubbornness. No. Forgiving was easy when given the legitimate chance at a World Series title.

Indians fans' loyalty reached a pinnacle in 1995. Never before had their emotions risen and poured onto the field in such feverish delight. This was it. The Moment had arrived, a little late perhaps, but never had their been a more welcome guest.

Baseball was back, and by God, the Indians were winning, winning, *winning!*

Behind every championship caliber team there is a brilliant GM. Hired as president and chief operating officer, as well as serving in the capacity of general manager, almost a year after the Jacobs brothers purchased the franchise in December of 1986, Hank Peters came to the Tribe with an impressive resume that spanned over 42 years in pro baseball. Prior to joining the Indians, he spent 12 seasons in Baltimore, where he was the executive vice president-general manager. The most important set of moves he made with Cleveland was assembling a front office second to none. It all started with his own clairvoyance in bringing Tom Giordano, John Hart, and Dan O' Dowd along with him from Baltimore. Giordano, who had worked alongside him the entire time both men worked for the Orioles, immediately became Peter's assistant.

Hart began his stint with the club in 1989 as a special assignment scout. By September 12 of that season, he replaced Doc Edwards as manager on an interim basis. For 19 games to be exact. This was done, Peters reasoned, so that Hart could better evaluate the team's talent. One year later, he was promoted to director of baseball operations. On September 18, 1991, he succeeded the soon to be retired Peters as general manager. The first home run hit by Hart was the deal that brought Kenny Lofton to the Tribe. Another important factor to the organization's plan for success was his realization that the best way to preserve the future was to sign a hoard of young players, such as Lofton, Belle, Baerga, and Nagy to extended contracts. This way, instead of losing players, the Indians were able to use free agency to their benefit. For his efforts, and since he shaped the team that turned around the club's fortunes, he was named the major league's Executive of the Year by *The Sporting News* following the strike-shortened '94 season. He also won the award in '95.

While directing the Indians farm system, O' Dowd, a former director of player development for the Orioles, proved to be a visionary when sorting through the multitude of minor league ball players and consistently finding a diamond in the rough. Under his tutelage, the organization quickly earned recognition as one of baseball's best when it came to player development. He later became director of baseball operations and Hart's right hand man.

Indeed, it was an executive team of the highest order. Of course, the gentlemen in the suits sitting in the box seats could do little to thwart the opposition once the Indians took the field. But they had little to worry about in 1995.

It became apparent early on that this was one of the greatest teams in franchise history. They possessed a knack for resurgence when all seemed lost in the final innings of a game. The Tribe came from behind to win 48 games in '95, including 27 last inning rallies. Each night it seemed was a new high watermark that provided larger than life moments. Manny Ramirez smacked a Dennis Eckersley slider over the left field wall for a 12th inning victory at Jacobs Field on July 16. Two days later, Belle faced Angels closer Lee Smith with one out, the bases loaded and his team trailing 5-3 in the bottom of the ninth inning. He worked the count to two balls and one strike before pulverizing a slider 425 feet for the dramatic win. The magic continued one week later, the next time the Indians faced Eckersley in Oakland and Smith in Anaheim, arguably the two best closers in baseball history. In both games, Cleveland rallied in their last at-bat to take the lead, and Jose Mesa slammed the door in the bottom half to preserve two more miracle wins.

The season started late due to the players' strike, but that did not slow down the Indians in their quest for 100 victories. Cleveland moved into a tie for first place in the Central Division on May 10. The next day, they held a half-game lead, and they never looked back. By the All-Star break, Cleveland owned a 12-game lead over the second place Kansas City Royals.

On the night of September 8, the Indians captured their first division title since 1954. It was the earliest clinching of a title since division play began in 1969. Cleveland's baseball relative from the south, the Reds, won their 1975 NL West title on the same day. Of course, if the season had begun on time, the Indians would easily have shattered that record.

One major league record they did hold at the end of the regular season was winning their division by the largest margin in history. The Tribe held a 30-game advantage over the Royals. And they did reach the century mark in wins, ending up with a 100-44 record. Their winning percentage of .694 stands as the 10th best in the modern era. Also broken was the franchise season attendance record. 2,842,725 people saw the Tribe play at Jacobs Field in '95, over 200,000 fans more than the previous mark set in 1948.

Just how dominant was the this team during their memorable run? They led the American League with a .291 batting average and team ERA at 3.83. No other team in the AL posted an ERA under 4.00. The normal starting lineup featured seven .300 or better hitters, led by Eddie Murray's .323 average. The Indians set a franchise record by belting 207 home runs. They scored 840 runs. The pitching staff combined for 10 shutouts and 926 strikeouts. Jose Mesa saved 46 games out of 48 opportunities. The starting rotation was led by Dennis Martinez (12-5) and Charles Nagy (16-6), and free agent pick up Orel Hershiser neared his 1988 Cy Young form by posting a 16-6 record.

No wonder the Boston Red Sox were overwhelmed in the three game Divisional Playoff series. The most trouble Cleveland had came in game one, but Tony Pena extended the late inning heroics of the regular season to the playoffs by blasting a 13th inning homer for a 5-4 victory. Following the series, the Tribe players were greeted by 2,000 fans upon their arrival at Hopkins International Airport in Cleveland. Well, that's normal for a playoff winner, right? Sure it is. But not at three in the morning.

Thankfully for the Indians, destiny couldn't stomach a fairy tale ending to the ALCS. The way the Seattle Mariners season had gone, it seemed like miracles were being pulled out of the players' tobacco pouches. They completed an amazing come-from-behind run in the final weeks of the regular season to overtake the California Angels for the AL West title. Of course, it never would have happened without a total collapse by the Angels. Wait a minute. Losing a double-digit lead in September is more like disappearing into thin air. Anyway, the Mariners did have Lady Luck in their dugout, but the Indians had a better team. Cleveland won in six games.

Next up were the National League champion Atlanta Braves in the Fall Classic. They had a pitching staff as stingy as a tightwad fallen on hard times. Unfortunately, throughout the Series, Atlanta's aces showed the nation how dominating they could be. Cleveland's staff was almost as good, but you know the old saying. Almost only counts if you're playing for the consolation prize and want to appear on *Regis & Kathie Lee* instead of *Good Morning America*. The Braves sent our hearts reeling by stopping the Tribe in six.

But, the good news was that spring training was only a few months away. Cleveland still had the best team in baseball.

So, in 1996, after the Indians cruised to the division title by winning 99 games, everyone cleared their dockets to ensure a seat in front of the tube, or if lucky enough, a seat at Jacobs Field, in order to root the Indians on to another shot at World Series glory. But first they had to handle the year's wild-card entrant, the Baltimore Orioles. No problem.

One thing many had difficulty swallowing was the fact that the Tribe had to travel to enemy territory for the first two games in the series. Cleveland ended up with the best record in baseball. Shouldn't the best team be given the early advantage? They earned it. The first two games should be played in the top team's ball park, the third and fourth in the underdog's backyard, and the fifth, if necessary, should go back to the first place team's home. It makes sense. Why should a wild-card team be given an edge?

Well, its too late now.

The Orioles won the first two games at Camden Yards, leaving the Indians in a deep hole. They struggled in their home opener, but pulled it out in dramatic fashion. Albert Belle hit a grand slam late in the game to turn the tide in the series. So it seemed.

Watching Roberto Alomar hit the series winning home run in game four was like seeing Superman being taken down by a problem child with a handful of kryptonite. Everyone on the planet had seen the video replay of Alomar's incident with home plate umpire John Hirschbeck in the final week of the season. Fans in Cleveland showed exactly how a multi-million dollar brat deserves to be treated when they turned their backs and sent down an avalanche of boos every time he came to the plate. If there was any kind of justice in baseball in 1996—better yet, if there was any kind of order in the commissioner's office—any one who blatantly disrespects the sport and all the children who watch and strive to be just like him someday and shows his immaturity by spewing saliva and germs on the man who regulates authority down on the field, should be dealt with severely and swiftly. This is not the NBA, and ball players are not Dennis Rodman. Alomar should have been forced to sit out the post-season. Why were the principals who run Baseball so paralyzed to take action, almost causing a walkout by the umpires during the playoffs? I know the ruling parties fashioned several excuses for their unwillingness to slap a stiff penalty on Alomar, but a meager five-game suspension, to be served at the beginning of the following season, in no way sufficed for such a temper tantrum. Albert Belle was reprimanded with a similar five-game suspension for his aggressive base running on Milwaukee's Fernando Vina earlier in the year. Most everyone who saw that play thought it was well within the confines of how to play the game. Insulting an umpire and a nation of fans is not.

In fact, Alomar's actions on that despicable night brought the former

Nice Guy into the spotlight as an antithesis of every professional athlete who is toted in hand by the almighty buck, and alienates himself from team spirit while waging a personal war for better statistics. It also may have been the only thing in all of baseball that made people forget about Marge Schott for a while. It also made Belle's halo look a little less tainted for once.

Who knows now? Maybe someone else would have stepped out of the Orioles dugout in Alomar's place and delivered the fatal blow instead. Over the years, the Indians have seldom had luck on their side. All the horseshoes ever hung up in the clubhouse immediately turned upside down, and the disaster of the '96 playoffs only legitimized that curse.

Many critics blamed the quick exit on some questionable decisions by manager Mike Hargrove, most of which centered on how he handled the pitching staff. Some claimed it was due to too much tinkering by Hart. Trading Mark Clark and signing an arm-weary Jack McDowell instead of Ken Hill comes to mind. So does the Baerga trade, even though Carlos struggled tremendously with the Mets. But the main reason was that the Indians bats, the same ones that produced the most runs in the league during the regular season, once again were silenced by good pitching. Plus the defense was shaky at times. Lofton lost a short fly ball in the sun that kept the O's ninth inning alive in game four, and allowed Alomar to tie the game with a base hit and eventually send it into extra innings.

Perhaps the frustration began to show after the '96 season. It was not supposed to end the way it did. The reigning sentiment of the most vocal fans was the Indians "owed" them a World Series title. Of course, there is always a certain amount of anger attached to something you love when that something seemingly betrays your emotions. Maybe there is even room for resentment. After all, everyone, including the entire organization believed the Indians would be back to claim victory in the Fall Classic.

It was practically expected. But we can't honestly say we're worse off for their efforts.

We should keep one thing in mind about the Indians teams of the 1990s. No matter what the outcome of those seasons were, they supplied their fans with one truly precious gift. Something that had stowed away many, many years ago on other teams' flights out of town.

The Indians gave us hope. At least for a few good seasons, we could smell the aroma of roasted peanuts at Jacobs Field and see the steam from hot dogs rising in the chilly night air of late October.

The Indians may not be as historically beloved as the New York Yankees. Today, they may not be America's Team, like the Atlanta Braves have been called by Ted Turner. But, hey. That's fine. They have a more intimate place in the hearts of their fans.

The Indians are Cleveland's team.

HISTORY
&
TRIVIA

I
MEMORABLE
SEASONS

1
Before 1900

Which came first, the chicken or the egg? Oh, I guess it really doesn't matter. Poultry is poultry whatever way you analyze it.

Right now, we'll concern ourselves with a less cosmically significant subject, yet one as equally argumentative, like the beginnings of professional baseball in Ohio's largest city.

Before the Indians original namesake, the Bluebirds, took to the field at the close of the 19th Century, Cleveland had been the stomping grounds for a number of teams. Though none of them erected a very memorable monument on the landscape of the sport, they had their moments, and more than likely helped pave the way for a well organized club to succeed. Somebody had to take the first steps, no matter how disastrous or unforgettable they may have been. If anything, the previous attempts shed a light on Cleveland and showed enough people that the Forest City was a true sports town.

One of the earliest teams was the Spiders, owned by Frank Robison. But they were not the first professional baseball team to call Cleveland home.

It is often customary that, with the passing of time, historical fact becomes deluded by heresy, by countless retellings or reprinting of events, each time a little different, with certain elements added or omitted. Or, contemporary historians will take liberties in revising actual occurrences, leaving us with loose accounts of a bygone era. With that in mind, there is some debate as to when exactly the first game involving a professional Cleveland nine took place. Some records claim that date to be June 2, 1869. What is known for certain is that the group fielded that day by the home team was the first Cleveland Base Ball Club. Their opponents were the Cincinnati Red Stockings, organized by former professional cricket player Harry Wright. Since the Red Stockings were the originators of paying every member on the team a salary for the sole reason of playing ball, and since it was public knowledge, they are recognized as the first ever professional baseball team. The Red Stockings initiated this practice at the start of the season of 1869. To remain competitive with the Cincinnati club, several teams immediately followed suit. Up until that time, many teams paid money to players for their service, but none openly admitted to paying every one on the roster.

The contest in question was played at Case Commons field in Cleveland where the Red Stockings won, 25-6. Though that score would say differently, such a lopsided loss was not disgraceful. The Red Stockings played in 57 games in '69. They won 56 of those outright, with the only black mark on their record that year being a tie.

Some references consider that Cleveland bunch to be the area's first pro team, since the players were offered payment for their services. Franklin Lewis, in his book on the history of the Indians, simply titled, *The Cleveland Indians*, published in 1949 by G. P. Putnam's Sons, denies that team professional status. It is his assessment that most of the players accepted the money, but a few refused. Since not all the players received compensation for their efforts in 1869, as well as in the following season, they should have been viewed as a semi-pro nine. His argument is supported by a newspaper listing of the day. *The New York Times* printed an article that named all the professional base ball clubs in the United States in 1869. Nowhere on that list was there a team hailing from Cleveland.

In order to pinpoint the next logical date for the birth of pro ball in Cleveland, a few more facts must be known. First of all, the National Association of Professional Base Ball Players (NAPBBP or NA for short) was founded in 1871, as a way to affiliate the various pro teams throughout the country. Though the NA had a hard time keeping teams to honor their schedules, it was the only organized effort around that was devoted solely to clubs that paid all their players. After the original Cleveland Base Ball Club joined the league, the fact that all the players on their roster were being paid became public knowledge for the first time.

Cleveland's first game as a member of the NA was played on May 4, 1871. Most references consider this to be the precise birthday of the city's pro game. The reference volume *Total Indians* (from the editors of *Total Baseball: The Official Encyclopedia of Major League Baseball*) is one source that cites the game played on that day as being accurate. That may be taking the easy way out. It is a date immune to local myth and secrecy. The history books are clear on that. Still, one can't help but wonder if, during the '69 and '70 seasons, the team just failed to accurately report its payroll.

So, like the whole chicken or egg mystery, the debate about Cleveland's first professional game rages on.

Trivia Questions

1. What was the first professional base ball franchise in Cleveland called?

2. How many years did they play in the National Association?

3. Where did the Cleveland team play that "first" pro game on May 4, 1871?

4. What was the outcome of the game that day?

5. What was the date of the club's home opener in their first season of National Association play?

6. That game, played against Chicago, ended in the eighth inning with Cleveland behind, 11-6. Why was the game prematurely halted?

7. For the 1871 season, Cleveland played a total of 29 games. How many did they win?

8. What was the club's record in 1872?

9. In 1879, the National League, in its third year of existence, added a franchise in Cleveland, bringing their total number of teams to eight. Who was responsible for organizing the franchise, then petitioning the NL for membership?

10. What was the nickname of this National League Cleveland franchise?

11. What year did the NL club disband?

12. In what season did the NL club finish 47-37, to post their best record ever, and finish in third place in the standings?

13. This Cleveland pitcher led the NL in victories that same year with 45, as well as in complete games (72) and innings pitched (657⅔). Two seasons later, he again led the league with 36 wins and 65 complete games in 595⅔ innings. Who was he?

14. On June 12, 1880, Cleveland played against the Worcester Brown Stockings in a National League contest. Worcester pitcher J. Lee Richmond was the first pitcher to accomplish what feat in that game?

15. What major league record did Cleveland pitcher Dave Rowe set on June 24, 1882?

16. In 1889, the NL again welcomed a franchise to Cleveland. This team, called the Blues, originated two years before as members of a

rival league. They transferred to the NL when the Detroit Wolverines Base Ball club folded. What was the name of the league they played in prior to joining the NL?

17. After joining the National League the Blues changed their name to the Cleveland Spiders. How many seasons did they play in the NL?

18. In order to create a post-season in 1892, the NL regular season was split with the first half winner meeting the second half winner in a "World Series" to determine the league (and world) champion. Who did Cleveland play for the title in '92?

19. What was the outcome of the '92 "World Series"?

20. The divided season concept was abandoned after the '92 season. Instead, in '94, a new trophy was presented to the winner of a seven game series between the first and second place teams at the end of the NL's regular season. What was this trophy called?

21. Who was the trophy named after? How long did the new format for determining the world champion last?

22. What years did the Spiders play for the aforementioned trophy?

23. At the end of their last season as a member of the National League, the NL bought out the Cleveland Spiders. How much did the NL pay to get the Spiders out of the league?

24. The 1899 season was a disaster. That year the Spiders managed to register the worst record in major league history. What was their win-loss record for the season?

25. In 1890, a year after the Spiders became affiliated with the National League, a fourth pro club came to Cleveland. This was the only time in the city's baseball history that it was home to two different pro franchises in the same season. The circuit this team

belonged to was called the Players League. The Players League was, as the name suggests, organized by former National League and American Association players who were upset with the system and set out on their own in an attempt to steal some the NL's and AA's popularity. The league lasted for one season. What was the nickname of the Cleveland franchise?

2
The First Season

O n the day Cleveland became an official Major League ball club in 1901, the Blues were, quite due to the imposition of nature, handed one of Baseball's all-time honors. They participated in the first game ever played in American League history. The other three games scheduled were rained out.

Remember, in the season of 1900, the newly christened American League was still considered a minor league, thus the Blues were a minor league team that year. They finished the season with a 63-73 record, good for sixth place, and 19½ games behind the first place Chicago White Sox. So, 1900 was more or less a practice run, a means of building up regional followings. One year later, Ban Johnson, the league's president, declared the AL to be a major league. Therefore, the year of 1901 is recognized as the beginning of the American League. It is also the birth year of the team we now call the Cleveland Indians.

Trivia Questions

1. What was the date of the first Major League game played by the Blues?

2. Who were the Blues opponents that day?

3. Where was the game played?

4. Who led off the game for the Blues, thus becoming the first batter in American League history?

5. Who was the starting pitcher for Cleveland that day?

6. What was the outcome of the game?

7. Name the winning pitcher in the Blues' 10-4 victory on April 27, 1901, the team's first win ever.

8. Name the team Cleveland played in their home opener at League Park on April 29, 1901.

9. What was the final score of that game?

10. Who was the winning pitcher in that game?

11. Who was the Blues manager in 1901?

12. The manager named in the previous answer left Cleveland the next season. What team did he go on to manage for the next eight seasons?

13. How many games did the aforementioned manager play in for the Blues during their inaugural season?

14. How many runs did the Blues score in the bottom of the ninth to beat the Washington Senators on May 23, 1901?

15. Who was the team's president from the first year of operation until 1910?

16. Name the team that turned a triple play against the Blues on September 26, 1901.

17. What was Cleveland's won-lost record in '01?

18. Name the pitcher who posted the most wins (16) for the Blues in their first season.

19. This pitcher lost 26 games in 1901. Four of the defeats came while he pitched for Milwaukee at the beginning of the year. Name him.

20. Name the player who led the Blues in batting in 1901 with a .321 average.

3
Title Hopes
(1908)

For the first seven seasons, the closest Cleveland came to winning a pennant was two third-place finishes, in 1903 and 1906. Despite being considered one of the best teams in the American League after the arrival of Napoleon LaJoie in 1902, the Naps, as the team was now called, failed to reach 90 wins until the season of 1908. That was the year Cleveland found themselves in the thick of the AL pennant race with two other clubs going into the final week of the season. It was a close race throughout the year. At the beginning of June, the Naps were in fifth place with a 19-18 record. Three victories later, Cleveland was in first. By September, it was obvious that the 1908 American League title race would go down in history as one of the most memorable finishes of all-time.

Trivia Questions

1. Before the season began, Hughie Jennings, manager of the Detroit Tigers, offered a trade to Naps owner Charles Somers. Who was the

player Jennings wanted to deal to Cleveland?

2. What Naps player did Jennings want in return?

3. What was the reason Jennings gave for wanting to trade the player referred to in question #1?

4. What incredible feat did the Naps perform in the fifth inning of a 15-6 victory over the Boston Red Sox on June 9, 1908?

5. On September 18 of that year, this Naps pitcher threw a no-hitter to beat the Red Sox 2-1. Name him.

6. A Cleveland newspaper credited the fine performance mentioned in the previous question to a lucky Egyptian amulet the pitcher bought the night before. The pitcher kept it in his pocket the entire time he was on the mound during the no-hitter. According to the newspaper, what was the cost of the amulet?

7. The Naps defeated the White Sox 1-0 on October 2. Who pitched a perfect game for Cleveland that day?

8. Who led the league with a minuscule 1.16 ERA in 1908?

9. What two teams along with Cleveland were involved in the pennant race on the final week of the season?

10. The AL title was not decided until the final series of the season, with all three teams still contending. What team ended up winning the 1908 American League pennant? What was the margin of victory that separated the first place team from the second and third place teams?

4
Good-bye, Nap (1914)

T his was the year Cleveland said so long to Nap Lajoie, following perhaps the most tumultuous season in the team's history. One year later they were re-named the Indians. Lajoie, who as player-manager of the Naps was the highest paid American Leauger at $10,000 a season, resigned from his dugout duties and offered to take a pay cut in '09. James McGuire took over as manager, then resigned in 1911.

The changes at the top did little to motivate the team, and Cleveland's highest finish following their legendary run in '08 was an 86-win season in 1913, which left them in third place. I get the feeling that fans would have been grateful for a repeat of that performance in 1914, as attendance for the season would show. Not since the first year of the American League did so few come to see their Cleveland base ball club play.

Trivia Questions

1. How many games did the Naps win in 1914?

2. How many losses did they suffer that year?

3. Who was the Naps manager during the dreadful campaign?

4. The season was so bad that the Naps finished in last place. How many days during the season were the Naps not in last place?

5. How many games behind the first place Philadelphia Athletics did Cleveland finish?

6. On July 11, the Naps lost to the Boston Red Sox, 4-3. What first year pitcher won that game for Boston?

7. What milestone did Lajoie reach during the season?

8. What was Lajoie's batting average for his final season with Cleveland?

9. Who decided to transfer the minor league Toledo team of the American Association to Cleveland for the 1914 season?

10. What was the total home attendance figure for Naps games in 1914?

5
Pennant Fever (1921 and 1926)

Playing the role of the favorite has never been a tailor-made part for the Cleveland Indians. Predicted to win the AL pennant at least a handful of times during their first two decades, the team always found ways to make the prognosticators seem whimsical, even foolish. All the disappointment came to an end in 1920. (More on that later.) But a new obstacle was immediately shoved in the way. Could Cleveland repeat as champions of the baseball world?

Following their pennant runs in 1920 and '21, the Tribe slumped for four straight seasons, placing fourth in '22, third in '23, and sixth in '24 and '25. The most wins collected during that span was 82 (1923), and the most losses was 86 (1924). Come the season of '26, the Indians were gearing up for another run. Little did anyone know it would be the last time until 1940 that the Tribe would be contenders. It was the exact opposite of the 1921 spring training: Cleveland was expected to go nowhere. Even the fans' optimism, at a frenzied peak a few seasons ago, began to wane. Lucky for the Indians, a good old-fashioned pennant race was just what the baseball gods ordered.

Trivia Questions - 1921

1. The Indians had to fight through misfortune the entire season. Injuries were the main culprit early on. Name the Tribe's every day second baseman who suffered a broken arm in spring training and missed the first quarter of the season.

2. Name the Indians catcher who broke his finger before the start of the season opener and was unable to play again until July 15.

3. The tail-end of Cleveland's schedule was brutal to say the least. How many consecutive games did the Tribe play on the road to close out the season?

4. Who collected seven extra base hits in a row during a doubleheader against the St. Louis browns on September 5?

5. The most crucial blow of the season came during a game on September 11 when this Tribe legend tore ligaments in his right knee and was lost for the remainder of the year. Name him.

6. Despite all the injury problems, Cleveland was in first place on September 16, after this pitcher beat the Washington Senators, 2-0, while allowing only four hits. The Tribe hurler in question went on to win 16 games for the season, even though his ERA was 4.01. Who was he?

7. The key series of the season came on the days of September 23-26. The Indians were locked in a battle for first place with the famed New York Yankees. Where was the series played?

8. What team won three of the four games in the series and eventually ended up winning the AL pennant of 1921?

9. Name the legendary player who hit at a .721 pace for the series (8 for 11). Hint: This player hit a then major league record 59 homers in 1921.

10. The Indians did not have a regular starter hit below .285 in 1921. Tris Speaker led the team with a .362 average. What was the team's overall batting average for the season?

Trivia Questions - 1926

1. This Indians player became the last pitcher in Major League history to win two complete games in a doubleheader on August 28. He beat the Red Sox, 6-1, in the first game, then, 5-1, in the second. Name him.

2. How old was George Burns when he was named the AL's Most Valuable Player for the 1926 season?

3. How many doubles did he hit that year, setting a new Major League record?

4. Name the only pitcher on the 1926 Cleveland staff who had remained with the Indians from the 1921 squad.

5. The key matchup of the '26 season began on September 15. It was a six-game series at Dunn Field. Who were the Tribe's opponents in the series?

6. How big of a lead did the team mentioned in the previous answer hold over the Indians going into the series?

7. How many games did the Indians win in the series?

8. So which team ended up winning the 1926 AL pennant and by how many games?

9. At the end of the season, two baseball immortals retired from their respective teams: Tris Speaker from the Indians and Ty Cobb from the Tigers. The timing of their retirement caused many to speculate that they were forced out of the game, due to allegations that they had agreed to throw a contest between the Indians and Tigers back in 1919. It had been claimed by a former Tiger player that Cobb, Speaker, and Dutch Leonard, also of the Tigers, and Smoky Joe Wood of the Indians, all put money down on the game, which the informant alleged was deliberately lost by Cleveland. The Indians were already assured of a second place finish at the time, the player claimed, so the game had no bearing on the outcome of the standings. Who was the informant to this alleged scandal?

10. What was the outcome of baseball commissioner Kenesaw Mountain Landis' investigation into the matter?

6
Mutiny
on the Diamond
(1940)

I t was a season of promise, the pact between a baseball team and its city of fans being made on opening day when Bob Feller took the mound and was initiated into immortality. Ultimately though, it became a season of uprising, one that branded the Indians with a despicable reputation.

Though they finished 15 games or better above .500 for five straight seasons during the previous decade, the Tribe never seriously threatened the American League powerhouses of the day, namely the New York Yankees. The team's closest finish to first place over that span was 12 games back. Considered to be only good enough to finish a distant third behind Boston and New York at the conclusion of spring training in 1940, Cleveland surprised the so-called experts and challenged for the top spot the entire year. This time, their nemesis was the Detroit Tigers.

They battled for six games at the end of September, including the final series played in Cleveland, which determined who became American League Champions.

Trivia Questions

1. The season opener was played on April 16 at Comiskey Park. What feat did Feller accomplish against the White Sox that day?

2. The Indians won the opener, 1-0. Name the player who scored the only run of the game and the player who batted him in.

3. Feller had an amazing year. He led the AL in six pitching categories, including wins and strikeouts. How many victories did he record during the season, and how many batters did he fan?

4. On June 13, following a 9-5 defeat at the hands of the Red Sox the day before, a crucial loss that dropped Cleveland into third place, the Tribe players revolted. Half the team visited club president Alva Bradley, requesting that he immediately fire their manager. The players cited the manager's constant bickering and criticizing of key members of the team as crippling their chances to win the pennant. They told Bradley they could only win the AL if they had another manager. No immediate action was taken by Bradley and the manager remained. Who were the players trying to oust?

5. Who did the players recommend as his replacement?

6. That incident caused the Indians to be called by a less than flattering nickname the remainder of the season. What was the nickname?

7. In response to all the ridicule the players received from baseball fans and the media across the country, they agreed to sign a statement retracting their demand to have their manager fired. The statement,

signed by 21 of the players on the roster, was printed in three city newspapers on June 17, 1940. Name the four players who did not sign the statement.

8. After being tossed out of a game, owner Bradley promised this player a $500 bonus if he could finish the season without being ejected from another game. Name the player.

9. Going into the final series against the Tigers, Cleveland needed a three game sweep to win the pennant. Feller started the first game for the Tribe, while Detroit named a surprise starter, a 30-year-old rookie who had won only two games in his career. Unfortunately, the Tigers won the game, 2-0, thanks to a home run by Rudy York which barely made it over the left field fence. Can you name the obscure pitcher who beat the Indians and won the American League pennant for the Tigers that day?

10. How many games did the Indians win to finish one game behind Detroit in 1940?

Ray Narleski

PITCHER CLEVELAND INDIANS

Mickey Vernon

1st BASE CLEVELAND INDIANS

Vic Wertz

1st BASE CLEVELAND INDIANS

jim piersall

CLEVELAND INDIANS
OUTFIELD

7
The Day
Cleveland Cried
(1960)

We all have favorite players. Those who captivate our imaginations and allow our spirits to soar. We put all our faith in the webbing of their gloves, in the heart of their bats. For someday, we believe, they will lead our team to victory in the World Series.

Unless they are unceremoniously jettisoned to another ball club right when our anticipation has reached a zenith. It is then that we realize a part of us is lost forever the moment he leaves town.

In 1960, Tribe fans felt the loss deep in their hearts, if not their spirit, Easter Sunday, April 17. The sun arose like any other day, but news that would have a far reaching impact on the future of the club blindsided most fans and left them groggy with disbelief. How could "Trader" Lane, the team's general manager, be so unsympathetic? How would the Tribe win without their best player?

The fans would blame this one deal for bringing an abrupt end to the franchise's golden era and opening the door to a pennant famine the size of Ohio.

How could Cleveland say good-bye to Rocky Colavito?

Trivia Questions

1. The day Colavito was traded, the Indians were playing the White Sox in an exhibition game in Memphis, Tennessee. In his first at bat, Rock hit a home run. In the fourth inning, he reached first on a fielder's choice. After he returned to the dugout, who had the task of informing Colavito that he had been traded?

2. How many days before the '60 season opener did the trade occur?

3. What team was Rock traded to?

4. Who was he traded for?

5. How many seasons did the player Colavito was traded for play with Cleveland?

6. What was the player's batting average for the Indians in 1960?

7. What position did Colavito play for Cleveland?

8. How many homers did he hit in the year before he was traded?

9. How many HRs did he hit during his four full seasons with the Tribe before the trade?

10. What team did Cleveland open the season against in 1960?

11. Five days before the Colavito trade, Frank Lane had dealt an

Indians player to Detroit. Name the player traded to the Tigers and the player the Indians received in the deal.

12. Lane wasn't done pulling off shocking trades. On August 3, he completed another deal with the Tigers. This time, it did not involve any players. See if you can guess the two men who were moved in the trade.

13. Who became interim manager of the Indians for one day on August 3, 1960, then was released from the team five days later, only to join the Tigers as a coach?

14. At the end of the year, Lane's contract with Cleveland expired. Name the organization that then hired him to serve as executive vice-president and general manager.

15. In his three seasons as GM of the Indians, how many deals did "Trader" Lane make?

16. What team was Harvey Kuenn traded to on December 3, 1960, during the annual winter meetings?

17. That month also featured an expansion draft, with the Los Angeles Angels (later renamed the California Angels, then the Anaheim Angels) and Washington Senators selecting seven Cleveland players for their rosters. Name two of the players claimed.

18. How many home runs did Colavito hit for Detroit in '60? '61? '62? '63?

19. Actually, 1960 was not the end of Colavito's career with the Tribe What year was he traded back to Cleveland?

20. The Rock played a little over two more seasons with Cleveland, clouting 61 homers before being dealt to the White Sox. In hindsight, some experts consider the re-acquisition of Colavito to be a blown

deal, considering who they gave the Chicago White Sox in order to
get Colavito. What team sent Colavito to the White Sox so they could
send him to the Tribe as part of a three way trade?

8
Happy Hour at the Stadium (1974)

he bottom fell out in 1960. First for the team, with the Rocky Colavito trade, then in the standings, where it seemed the Cleveland Indians were hanging by a rope, and every season that rope let out a little more slack. Even the few times they did manage to somehow climb above a .500 winning percentage, there was very little enthusiasm. I guess that was warranted. Because from 1960 to 1993, the Tribe finished in fourth place or lower every season except in '68. That year they were third with 86 wins and 75 losses. Yet, they were still 16½ games out of first place. Quite often, Cleveland finished in sixth place or worse. Maybe only the most devout baseball fans in the city were even aware that, yes, there still was a post-season format to determine the champion of the sport.

That's not to say the Indians didn't have some memorable players on their roster from time to time. Gaylord Perry pitched in Cleveland in 1972-75. Jimmy Piersall was a member of the team for three years in 1959-61. There was some young talent, too. Players that went on to play in their prime with other ball clubs: Luis Tiant, Graig Nettles, Buddy Bell, to name some. These players may have helped win some games, but the Indians were still one of baseball's drabbest franchises.

Sometimes it seemed like the organization would try anything in its never ending quest to bring in a crowd. One time in particular, a "revolutionary" promotion backfired. Which brings us to the season of '74.

Trivia Questions

1. Name the former Indians player who was fired as coach, along with Warren Spahn and Joe Lutz at the beginning of the season.

2. The three men who replaced them were Tony Pacheco, Clay Bryant, and a former Tribe player from the golden '50s. Name him.

3. On April 27, Indians GM Phil Seghi traded away a promising first baseman, who went on to help the New York Yankees win a pennant in 1976. He was a member of the Tribe from 1971-74, and won the AL Rookie of the Year Award in '71. Name him.

4. Name the player Cleveland purchased on waivers from the California Angels late in the season.

5. How many home runs did the player in the previous answer hit during his 21 year major league career?

6. The player referred to in the last two questions signed a contract worth $180,000 for the upcoming '75 season. This irked Indians pitcher Gaylord Perry whose contract paid him $150,000 in 1974. Perry was quoted as saying that he would have to renegotiate his contract, so he would be making more than the Indians new

acquisition. How much more than this player did Perry say he expected to make?

7. What two pitchers led the Tribe in wins in '74?

8. In an attempt to bolster attendance, the Indians and Cleveland Stadium offered a "beer night" promotion. 25,134 spectators showed up for the game played on June 4, where cups of beer were sold at an extra cheap price. How much were unlimited cups of beer sold for that night?

9. Who were the Indians opponents for the "beer night" game?

10. How did this promotion backfire, and what was the outcome of the game?

9
New Power Surge (1986)

C ertainly we remember these names from a bygone era? Pat Tabler. Cory Snyder. Tony Bernazard. Mel Hall. Maybe not. They're not exactly a "Who's Who in Baseball", or even Cleveland Indians baseball for that matter. That's not to say these or any other players who performed on the diamond in 1986 weren't good.

In fact, the Indians forgot their role as perennial stepping stones for the rest of the American League and provided their opposition with some stiff competition that year. They may not have threatened for the title, but Tribe batters led the AL in several offensive categories. Some of the players on the team were burgeoning stars and others had career years never again duplicated.

One thing was for certain: the Indians were an exciting team, leading many "experts" and analysts to predict an AL championship for Cleveland the following year. They came up considerably short, but that doesn't diminish their accomplishments in '86. Besides, the season also marked the beginning of the end of the franchise's lack of success. On

July 2 of the year, the Indians were sold to the Jacobs brothers, and an imminent metamorphosis was under way.

Trivia Questions

1. How many wins did the Tribe post during the season?

2. What was their American League leading team batting average for the season?

3. The Indians also led the league in run production. How many runs did they score in '86?

4. Who led the team with 29 home runs and 121 RBIs?

5. How many Tribe starters with enough plate appearances to qualify hit over .300 for the year?

6. Name those hitters.

7. Pitching was the team's main weakness all year long, as the staff accumulated a 4.58 ERA. What starting pitcher had a team low ERA of 3.51?

8. Who led the Indians in victories with 16?

9. He was the Tribe's starting centerfielder in '86, as well as the previous year, and in '87. In 1988, he signed a free agent contract with the San Francisco Giants. Name him.

10. What pitcher made his major league debut in August of '86, and went on to win five games in nine starts that season, then pitched for Cleveland through the '91 season, compiling a total of 60 wins in that span?

II
WORLD SERIES

Introduction

In professional sports, bringing a title to the home town will set off an explosion of euphoria, proving an old adage we learned the moment our sense of competition developed. *Everyone loves a winner*.

It also means that if you don't have season tickets, you'd better hustle on over to the nearest furniture store and find yourself a comfortable Lazy-boy to put in front of the TV set, because what the saying fails to tell us is that it gets awfully crowded on the bandwagon when the entire town falls in love with a champion. Over the years—over the *decades*—championships have been a rare occurrence in Cleveland, but nonetheless precious.

The Indians have played in four World Series. The first time was in 1920, under the stewardship of player-manager Tris Speaker, who led by example, carrying a big stick and swinging it with authority. His .388 batting average and 107 RBIs in the regular season would convince anybody of that. More important was his ability to hold the team together and keep them focused amid the Ray Chapman tragedy.

The next time the Indians appeared in the Series, they had a considerably different personality. Owner Bill Veeck had a reputation to create excitement, and he proved it by repeatedly shaking up the foundations of the club through his almost impulsive habit of wheeling and dealing, and his sense of promoting, which many have cited as the origin of the commercialization of baseball. Regardless of all the moves off the field, he came up with the right formula in 1948. This time the Indians player-manager was Lou Boudreau, who, like Speaker, was a true artist with the bat. He hit .355 in the regular season, and added 18 dingers and more than 100 RBIs. He could not have made it to the Series without an ace pitching staff that heralded two 20-game winners. Still, it was Boudreau, the regular season's MVP, who became the city's undisputed hero during the American League's first ever pennant playoff.

In 1954, the Tribe established a franchise record for most wins in one season. A phenomenal pitching staff recorded a league low 2.78 ERA. Larry Doby, the AL's first African-American player, led the league in home runs and RBIs. By winning the American League that season, Cleveland put a halt to the New York Yankees five-year monopoly on the pennant. So, the '54 Indians were considered by many to be one of the best teams ever assembled. It was going to be a rout in the Fall Classic that year.

Right. On paper it would have been.

That's why they play the games.

Certainly the story of the '95 Indians would have a happy ending. The Great Director sitting in his chair somewhere behind the scenes of the baseball world would stick to a formula that the audience was craving. Well, somewhere along the way the production was botched. The Atlanta Braves were cast in the role of the villains.

They should have rewritten the Cincinnati Reds into the script.

1
1920

1. How many victories did Cleveland claim during the regular season?

2. How many games did they lose?

3. The race for the AL pennant was a season long battle between Cleveland and the Chicago White Sox, culminating in the final series played at the beginning of October. Nursing a one-game lead, Cleveland played Detroit for five games, while Chicago played three against the St. Louis Browns. Seven of the Chicago players on the roster (along with a former player) were suspended by White Sox owner Charles Comiskey. Chicago was forced into using some of their reserves for the final series, and dropped two of the three contests. Cleveland won three games against the Tigers to finish two up on the Sox. Many believed that the Tribe had the pennant handed to them due to Chicago's misfortune. Why were the players suspended?

4. All right, so Speaker had an amazing year. But it was a "rebound" year for him. What was his batting average the year before?

5. Who replaced Chapman at shortstop?

6. The player in the previous answer pulled a hamstring muscle in early September and the Indians were forced to purchase a replacement from the New Orleans farm club for $6,000. Who was the Indians new shortstop?

7. Who led the pitching staff in victories during the regular season with 31?

8. Name the pitcher who added 24 wins that year.

9. The Indians opponents in the '20 Series were the Brooklyn Dodgers (also known as the Robins in honor of their manager, Wilbert Robinson). What was Brooklyn's record during the regular season?

10. How many games were played in the World Series, and how many did Cleveland win?

11. Who pitched and won the opening game of the Fall Classic for Cleveland?

12. Name the two pitchers who threw complete games for Brooklyn in the second and third games.

13. What feat did Elmer Smith accomplish in the first inning of Game Five, becoming the first player in World Series history to do it.

14. What did Tribe second baseman Bill Wambsganss do in the fifth inning of that same game that no other player has ever duplicated as long as the World Series has been played?

15. Who became the first pitcher to hit a Series home run, also in the fifth game?

16. Name Cleveland's pitcher in Game Six. He blanked the Dodgers (Robins), 1-0, in the game.

17. What pitcher won three games for the Tribe during the Fall Classic?

18. On what holiday did the Indians clinch the Series?

19. What was the amount of prize money each Indians player received for their post-season victory?

20. How were the Tribe's uniforms different for the 1921 season?

2
1948

1.Name the baseball legend who Bill Veeck hired as vice-president and farm director of the team prior to the start of the season.

2. Who pitched a no-hitter for the Tribe on June 30, a 2-0 victory over the Detroit Tigers?

3. One of Veeck's most important—and at the time most criticized —maneuvers during the season came on July 7, when he purchased the contract rights of this 20-plus season veteran pitcher of the Negro League. Can you name the pitcher?

4. What Negro League team was his contract purchased from?

5. The pitcher mentioned in the two previous questions went through a "secret" tryout at Cleveland Stadium. He threw 20 pitches before being tested by an Indians hitter. Who was the batter this pitcher faced?

6. How many games did the pitcher start for the Tribe in '48? How many wins did he post? How many shutouts? What was his team

leading ERA for the season?

7. Cleveland was at or near the top of the standings the entire year. A 7-1 loss to Detroit in the final game of the season left the Indians tied for first place with another club. To determine the champion of the AL, as well as what team would represent the league in the World Series, the first ever one-game playoff was contested on October 3. Who did the Tribe play that day, and where was the game played?

8. Who did Lou Boudreau select as his starter for the game?

9. Boudreau hit two home runs in the game, helping the Tribe to an 8-3 victory. His performance prompted Veeck to comment to the media afterwards that the team didn't win the pennant in 1948. So, when did he claim the Tribe actually won it?

10. Can you name the two 20-game winners on the Indians pitching staff that year?

11. Who led the team with 32 home runs?

12. Who was the Indians opponent in the 1948 Fall Classic?

13. Name the two starting pitchers in Game One. What was the final score of the game?

14. In that game, Bill Stewart, the umpire who was positioned near second base, blew a call in the eighth inning that later resulted in the winning run being scored. What was this blown call?

15. Who were the Indians starters in Games Two and Three, and what were the final scores of the games?

16. Name the two Tribe heroes from Game Four, a 2-1 Cleveland victory.

17. Game Five set a then Major League single game attendance record. How many spectators showed up to witness the game at Cleveland Stadium?

18. Who connected for two home runs on the opposing team in Game Five, resulting in an 11-5 defeat for the Indians?

19. The Tribe held a 4-1 lead in the eighth inning of Game Six. Bob Lemon loaded the bases with one out, and Boudreau decided to bring in a reliever. Who did he call on to try and get the Indians out of the jam? What was the outcome of the game?

20. Name the four Indian players who hit home runs in the Series.

JOHNNY ROMANO
Catcher

Cleveland
Indians

JOHNNY TEMPLE
Second Base

Cleveland
Indians

BUBBA PHILLIPS
Third Base-Outfield

Cleveland
Indians

GARY
BELL
CLEVE INDIANS

3
1954

1. How many games did the Indians win during the regular season?

2. Name the player who won the AL batting championship with a .341 average.

3. What position did he play, and how many seasons was he with the Tribe?

4. How many HRs did Larry Doby hit for the year? How many RBIs did he collect?

5. Name the five main starters in the Indians pitching rotation that year.

6. Which one of those pitchers started the most games in the AL that year (36) and which one threw the most complete games (21)?

7. The two pitchers in the previous answer also led the league in victories. How many wins did each of them have in the regular season?

8. How many complete games did the entire pitching staff record in the season?

9. What offensive category did Cleveland hitters lead the league in that year?

10. The Indians main competition throughout the season came from the New York Yankees. Cleveland started slow, going 3-9 at the beginning of the season. They quickly turned things around to take a half-game lead over New York at the All-Star break. Then the Tribe heated up down the stretch, putting together winning streaks of nine in a row in August and 11 in a row in the middle of September. Despite Cleveland's monster year, the Yankees weren't mathematically out of the race until the 18th of September. They ended up having an incredible season as well, making them the fourth team in major league history to accomplish this disappointing feat. What was it?

11. Who played third base for the Indians in '54, and how many seasons did he play with the club?

12. Indians GM Hank Greenberg made some key acquisitions during the season that helped catapult Cleveland to their record year. One of the best acquisitions was an outfielder from Baltimore who moved to first base for the Indians, after knee problems shelved Luke Easter. Who was this player?

13. What did the player from the previous answer do after Cleveland clinched the AL title on September 18, causing national newspapers to print a photo of him?

14. What National League team was considered to be the big underdog in the '54 Series versus the Indians?

15. What was the Indians' World Series opponent's record during the

regular season?

16. The Series started out the way many believed it would, with Cleveland scoring two runs in the first inning, on a two-out triple by Vic Wertz, but the offense stalled throughout the rest of the game. With the score tied in the top of the eighth inning 2-2, the turning point in the game, as well as in the Series, occurred when Willie Mays made a basket catch over his left shoulder, with his back to the plate, on a tremendous shot by a Cleveland batter with two on and no outs. The Indians failed to score, and lost the game 5-2 in 10 innings. Who was the victim of Mays's all-time highlight reel catch?

17. Who hit the game winning three-run homer for the Tribe's opponents in the opener, and how long was the shot?

18. Name the player from the opposing team who drove in two runs in the second game, on a single and a home run, to help his team beat the Indians, 3-1.

19. Who was the only Indian player to hit safely in every game played in the '54 World Series?

20. What was the final outcome of the Series?

3rd BASE

MAX ALVIS

PITCHER

TED ABERNATHY

OUTFIELD

VIC DAVALILLO

2ND BASE

LARRY BROWN

4
1995

1. Name five of the seven Indian regulars who hit for a .300 or higher batting average in '95.

2. How many home runs did Albert Belle hit in the month of September, equaling a Major League record held by Babe Ruth?

3. How many stolen bases did Kenny Lofton have during the regular season to lead the AL?

4. How many Major League games did Jose Mesa save during his career prior to the '95 season?

5. Mesa saved 38 games in as many opportunities before finally blowing one. What Detroit Tigers outfielder hit a home run off Mesa to end the streak on August 25?

6. What team did Cleveland beat on September 8 to clinch the AL Central title?

7. Who caught the final out of that game?

8. Was cork found in Albert Belle's bat after it was confiscated by AL authorities following his 11th inning game tying home run in the first game of the Divisional Playoffs against the Red Sox?

9. Tribe pitchers had an amazing series against Boston in the Divisional Playoffs, compiling a 1.74 ERA in the three-game sweep. How many hits did the heart of the Red Sox order, Mo Vaughn and Jose Canseco, get in 27 total at-bats in the series?

10. Who was the emergency starter and winner for Seattle in Game One of the ALCS?

11. Who had the most hits (11) for Cleveland in the ALCS?

12. What Indians pitcher won two games in the ALCS?

13. In Game One of the World Series, Greg Maddux threw a complete game for the Braves. How many pitches did he throw the entire game?

14. Who hit the sixth inning homer for Atlanta in Game Two that proved to be the difference in the final score?

15. Whose 11th inning single in Game Three provided the Indians with their first win of the Series?

16. What were the final scores of the six games in the '95 World Series?

17. Who were the two starting pitchers for Game Six?

18. Cleveland had one hit in Game Six. Who got the hit, a broken bat single, in the sixth inning?

19. Who hit the sixth inning home run for Atlanta in the final game,

which ended up being the Series clinching hit?

20. Who was the Tribe relief pitcher who surrendered that Series winning home run?

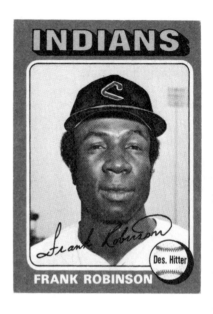

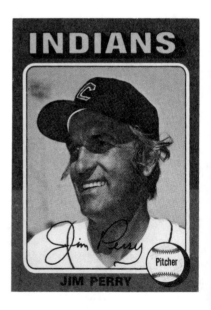

III
PERSONNEL
DEPARTMENT

1
Position Players

1. How old was Sandy Alomar, Jr., when he signed his first Major League contract with the San Diego Padres?

2. What Major League teams did Sandy's father play for during a 15-year career?

3. After being traded from the Indians, this catcher spent two years with Toronto before being traded to Houston where he stayed for 11 seasons. In Houston, he tied a National League record by catching three no-hitters. Name him.

4. What baseball league did former Indians second baseman Bobby Avila become president of?

5. Who hit a right-handed and left-handed home run in the same inning of a game in 1993?

6. This outfielder was signed by Cleveland after being released by Cincinnati in 1902. He ended up stealing a total of 165 bases during a seven-season career with Cleveland. Who was he?

7. This third baseman spent seven seasons with the Indians. In 1973, he led the AL in putouts at his position. He combined with his father to hit 407 major league home runs. Name him.

8. Speaking of father-son combinations, this Indians shortstop has been followed in the Majors by a son who played catcher for 19 seasons and by a grandson who turned into a pretty good second baseman. Who was he? Name his son and grandson.

9. What third baseman is acknowledged as the innovator of the now patented way to play a bunt, where the fielder picks up the ball bare-handed and throws to first base in one motion?

10. How many seasons was shortstop-second baseman Larry Brown with the Indians?

11. This former Indians first baseman turned an unassisted triple play against Cleveland on September 14, 1923, while playing for the Boston Red Sox. Who was he?

12. What team did the player mentioned in the previous question debut with in 1914? How many seasons did he play with the Tribe?

13. What season did Brett Butler lead the AL with 29 bunt hits?

14. This outfielder who played with Cleveland 1984-89 was voted College Player of the Year before being the second player selected in the 1981 amateur draft by the Chicago Cubs. Who was this?

15. Rico Carty was with Cleveland 1974-77. In 1960, when he began playing professional ball, he was converted from a catcher to an outfielder, though he later became a designated hitter with the Tribe. But the most interesting aspect of his becoming a professional was a dispute over the number of contracts he signed. How many different teams did he agree to terms with and what team was awarded his

playing rights?

16. Who was Leon Wagner platooned with in left field in 1967, prompting him to ask to be traded?

17. This centerfielder was considered to be a potential superstar by Indians president Gabe Paul. On June 12, 1963, the player was hit by a pitch and suffered a broken right arm. At the time of the injury, many considered him to be the top rookie of the season. He never made the impact that Paul expected and was traded to California in June of '68. Who was he?

18. According to Larry Doby himself, how many players would not shake his hand during his introduction to the team in the Cleveland clubhouse prior to his Major League debut on July 5, 1947 at Comiskey Park?

19. What team was Doby a member of before he became an Indian?

20. Who was the Indians regular shortstop 1972-77?

21. When this first baseman-outfielder was in the Negro League, he was referred to as "The Black Babe Ruth." Who was he?

22. Name the infielder who won the American League batting crown in 1929 with a .369 average.

23. What season did shortstop Julio Franco make his debut with Cleveland?

24. Name the player who would have won the AL batting title with a .363 average in 1959 if he had enough at-bats to qualify. He only had 399 plate appearances that season. Hint: his son played with Cleveland in 1988.

25. Who was the Indians first designated hitter in 1973?

26. This Indians outfielder became the first ex-Major Leaguer to step into the broadcast booth to do play-by-play announcing for Indians games. Who was he?

27. Who was the first batter ever to face Babe Ruth, when Ruth was a rookie pitcher for the Red Sox in 1914?

28. Who was Oscar Vitt referring to when he called this Indians outfielder the "best natural hitter I've seen since Joe Jackson?"

29. How many seasons did the player referred to in the previous question play for the Tribe? What was his lifetime batting average?

30. Who was the Indians starting catcher 1947-57?

31. What team was George Hendrick, an Indian 1973-76, a number one draft choice for in 1968?

32. This third baseman-second baseman batted over .300 for the Tribe in four straight seasons 1927-30. Who was he?

33. Before becoming an Indian in '63, this shortstop won the AL Rookie of the Year award with the Kansas City Athletics in 1961. Who was he?

34. Name the third baseman who hit .300 and added 32 homers in 1987.

35. What did Charlie Jamieson do twice in the same season, first during a game played on May 23, 1928, then on June 9?

36. How many seasons did Jamieson play with the Indians?

37. What were the odd circumstances involving third baseman Willie Kamm's retirement from playing the game?

38. Name the Indians third baseman who robbed Joe DiMaggio of hits in the first and seventh inning of the game played on July 17, 1941, which was the day Joltin' Joe's 56-game hitting streak came to an end.

39. What accomplishment did second baseman Duane Kuiper achieve on August 29, 1977?

40. Who was the Indians regular second baseman and served as Lou Boudreau's double play counterpart 1940-44?

41. What position did Rick Manning originally play when he was a number one draft choice in 1972?

42. Minnie Minoso played in 1,835 games during his major league career. How many did he play in a Cleveland Indians uniform?

43. Who was Cleveland's starting left fielder 1947-53?

44. Eddie Murray played baseball at Locke High School in Los Angeles. His younger brother Rich, who played briefly with the San Francisco Giants in the early '80s, was also on the high school squad. Can you name the Major League shortstop who also was a teammate of Murray's in high school?

45. What happened to Paul O' Dea on March 21, 1940?

46. Who played catcher for Cleveland 1911-1923?

47. Who played in the most games (137) for Cleveland in their first season?

48. How old was outfielder Vada Pinson when he joined the Indians in 1970, a season in which he led the team in hits (164), doubles (28), and RBIs (82)?

49. What four positions did Vic Power play during his stint with Cleveland 1958-1961?

50. Name the two Indians catchers who broke the "altitude catching record" on August 20, 1938. What exactly was the record?

51. What was Al Rosen's lifetime batting average in 1,044 games?

52. How many home runs did Rosen hit during his career in the majors?

53. 1953 was his best year in the home run department. How many balls did Rosen take over the fence that year?

54. Why did utility infielder Chico Salmon sleep with the lights on in his room?

55. Who hit three home runs, a triple, and collected eight RBIs in a game at Yankee Stadium on July 13, 1945?

56. How many seasons did catcher Luke Sewell play for the Tribe?

57. Who led the American League with 123 runs scored in 1955, while playing left field for the Indians?

58. This star of the 1984 U.S. Olympic team became the fourth player chosen in the amateur draft by Cleveland that year. Three times he hit over 20 home runs before departing to the White Sox in a trade. Who was he?

59. What did first baseman George Stovall become the first to do in 1914?

60. How many seasons did he play with Cleveland?

61. This player scored 36 points in the High School Conference Championship basketball game while he was enrolled at Limestone High School in Illinois. On a more current note, he belted 25 homers for the Tribe in '95 and outdid that by hitting 38 out in '96. Who is he?

62. How many home runs did Hal Trosky hit during his Indians career?

63. Besides Cleveland, what other team did Trosky play for?

64. How many seasons did Terry Turner wear a Cleveland uniform?

65. How many errors did Omar Vizquel commit in 624 chances at short in '95?

66. Who hit 20 triples in 1935?

67. What position did the player in the previous answer play, and how many seasons was he on the Tribe?

68. How many errors did the Indians commit as a team in 1901?

69. What was the first season Cleveland led the AL in fewest errors committed with 216?

70. What is the team's lowest error total for one season, and what year was it accomplished?

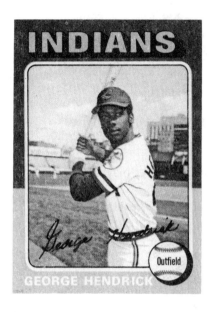

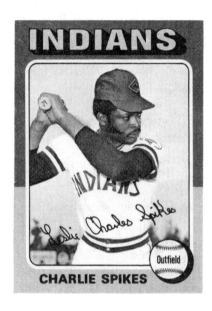

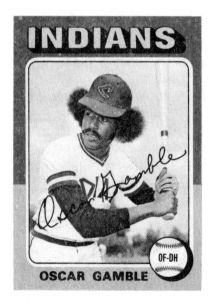

2

Pitchers

1. Why did Johnny Allen walk off the field in the second inning of a game at Fenway park on June 7, 1938?

2. Who forced Joe DiMaggio to ground into a bases-loaded double play in the eighth inning of the game in which the Yankee slugger's 56-game hitting streak was snapped?

3. Name the only father and son tandem to pitch for the Indians in their respective careers.

4. Who pitched a perfect game on May 15, 1981 against Toronto at Cleveland Stadium?

5. This former Indians pitcher (1958-67) won the home opener for the expansion Seattle Pilots in 1969. Who was he?

6. Who was Cleveland's first 20-game winner back in 1904?

7. In 1984, this pitcher finished third in the AL Cy Young Award voting. He was known as a master of the curve ball during a 21-year

Major League career, five of which were spent in Cleveland. Name him.

8. Who committed the throwing error in the fourth inning of what would have been a perfect game by Dick Bosman on July 19, 1974?

9. This reliever's fastball exceeded 95 miles per hour, but he preferred to throw off-speed pitches to try and fool batters. This habit of his to lay off the heat enraged manager Pat Corrales enough to come out of the dugout from time to time and order the pitcher to use his fastball. He set a then franchise record with 23 saves in 1984, but went down hill from there. Who was he?

10. This pitcher was a Tribe starter for six years. His best season came in 1986 when he posted 16 victories and threw 17 complete games. On June 27, 1991, he was traded to Toronto, then signed as a free agent with the Dodgers the following year. Name him.

11. This pitcher was renowned for his sinker. He suffered from a heart disorder that forced him out of the game in 1949. He spent just one season in Cleveland, but was the team's best reliever in 1948. Who was he?

12. How many hits did Rocky Colavito allow during his three inning pitching "career" with Cleveland in a game in 1958? How many base on balls did he surrender? How many runs did he give up?

13. What team did former Indians hurler John Denny win a Cy Young Award with in 1983?

14. How many games did Dennis Eckersley start while with the Indians 1975-77? How many games did he win in that stretch?

15. Cy Falkenberg's best year with Cleveland was in 1913. How many games did he win that season?

16. This pitcher won 13 consecutive decisions in 1930. He won 25 games that year. Who was he?

17. How many seasons in a row did the pitcher mentioned in the previous question win 20 or more games for the Tribe, starting with his first full season in 1929?

18. How many seasons did Mike Garcia pitch for the Indians, and how many victories and losses did he post during that stretch?

19. Name the pitcher who signed a then high-priced $2.3 million contract over 10 seasons in November, 1976, then suffered a torn rotator cuff at the end of his first season with the team and became a bust during the next few years.

20. Who was the last Tribe pitcher to throw 20-plus complete games in a season?

21. How many games did Vean Gregg win during his rookie campaign in 1911?

22. Why did Steve Gromek switch from playing shortstop to pitching in 1940?

23. Steve Hargan won 11 games for the Indians in 1970 and threw eight complete games. How many victories did he earn the following season?

24. After winning the Cy Young Award with the Los Angeles Dodgers in 1988, what did Orel Hershiser tell Johnny Carson he did to remain calm while on the mound?

25. During six seasons with Cleveland, this pitcher also played 50 games in the outfield. In 1906, he won 20 games. Who was he?

26. Name this first baseman-outfielder who made an appearance on

the mound in 1902 and is the only non-pitcher in Tribe history to lose a decision.

27. How many seasons did Willis Hudlin pitch for the Indians?

28. What was Hudlin's best season for victories?

29. How old was Doug Jones at the start of his rookie season in 1987?

30. Jim Kern, who pitched for Cleveland 1974-78 and again in 1986, spent nearly a season with Cincinnati in '82. Why was he traded from the Reds to the Chicago White Sox in August of that same year?

31. What pitcher representing Nicaragua in the 1973 amateur World Series , lost the championship game 1-0 in 10 innings to the United States?

32. What pitcher from 1961 to 1971 claims that he would have been a Hall of Famer if only he could have controlled a serious drinking problem that hindered his effectiveness?

33. What Major League record did Cal McLish equal on May 22, 1957, during a game versus the Boston Red Sox?

34. This pitcher finished second to Seattle's Randy Johnson in the AL Cy Young Award voting in 1995, and fourth in the MVP race. Name him.

35. Throughout a seven-plus season career with the Tribe, this pitcher was nagged by injuries, and was mostly sporadic. Still, he posted a team best 3.21 ERA in 1927 and won a career high 14 games in 1929. Who was he?

36. Acquired from the California Angels on May 11, 1977, this

pitcher posted earned run averages of 2.76 in 1978 and 2.40 the next season. He won 12 games in '79, while being the workhorse out of the bull pen. After spending time on three other teams, he was out of baseball by 1985. Name him.

37. What team beat Earl Moore by a score of 4-2 in 10 innings on May 9, 1901, a game in which Moore pitched the American League's first no-hitter through nine innings?

38. Who was named Louisiana "College Player of the Year" after leading the LSU Tigers to the National Championship in 1991?

39. Who led the AL with 130 base on balls allowed in 1945?

40. Before being signed by Cleveland the next month, what team was Dusty Rhoads released by in August of 1903?

41. How much did Cleveland sign Herb Score for in 1952?

42. Who fanned Babe Ruth more than any other pitcher during a 13 year career in the Majors, nine of which were spent in Cleveland?

43. In the Summer of '91, this pitcher led Team USA with five saves during the Pan American Games in Havana, Cuba. Who is he?

44. In 1960, Sonny Siebert threatened to quit the team unless he was allowed to try out as a pitcher. What were the two positions he played early in his minor league career, prior to becoming a successful hurler?

45. Who started the game in which Joe DiMaggio's 56-game hitting streak was snapped?

46. How many wins did Rick Sutcliffe post during his career with Cleveland 1982-84?

47. Luis Tiant spent six seasons with the Tribe 1964-1969. He pitched a four-hit shutout victory in his Major League debut, and went on to win 229 games in his career. Name the former Indians player who first signed Tiant to a pro ball contract.

48. George Uhle won 147 games for the Indians, while losing 119 during 10-plus seasons. One year before his professional career began in 1919, he pitched a Cleveland area team to the amateur baseball championship. What team was this?

49. Name the two pitchers fans selected to the all-time Indians Greatest Team, an honor that was voted for in 1969.

50. How many times have Cleveland starters thrown over 100 complete games in a single season?

3

Managers

1. Which Indians manager was an outfielder for the old National League Cleveland Spiders and batted .235 in his first year with that team?

2. Who was James McAleer's replacement for the Blues' second season?

3. How many games did Cleveland win under Napoleon Lajoie?

4. He was the youngest manager ever to open a season at just 24 years of age. Some of the people who ridiculed the move called him "the boy manager." Who was he?

5. Who has the most wins as manager of the Tribe with 728?

6. After Al Lopez resigned from managing the Indians following the 1956 season, what team did he become manager for on October 29 of that year?

7. Who did Hank Greenberg want to hire as Lopez's replacement,

where was this person working at the time, and why did the negotiations fall through?

8. What was former Indian pitcher Mel Harder's managing record with Cleveland?

9. This manager was hospitalized after suffering a heart attack during spring training in 1964. He returned in early July and continued managing the Tribe until he resigned on August 20, 1966. Name him.

10. This manager lost the tip of a finger on his right hand after it got caught on the bottom of a chair he angrily tossed in the San Francisco Giants clubhouse, the team he then managed. He was upset over his team's less than desirable play in a game during the '63 season. He became the Indians manager in 1968 and remained at that post until July of '71. Who was he?

11. This manager's playing career included stints in the Pacific Coast League, on the Washington Senators, Indians, California Angels, Milwaukee Braves, and Chicago Cubs. He ended his playing career in the Japanese Central League before managing several of Cleveland's farm teams. In 1972, he was promoted to head up the Indians. Who was he?

12. What Tribe manager won an MVP award in both the NL and AL as a player?

13. Who told the Indians he would not take the vacant manager's position unless Frank Robinson said it was okay?

14. Excluding John Hart's duties as interim manager in 1989, name the three managers who preceded Mike Hargrove.

15. What was Hargrove's lifetime batting average during his 12 year

Major League playing career?

16. What position did Hargrove play during his career?

17. Who has managed the Indians for the most seasons?

18. Who was Cleveland's last player-manager?

19. How many player-managers have the Indians had throughout their history?

20. Name half of them.

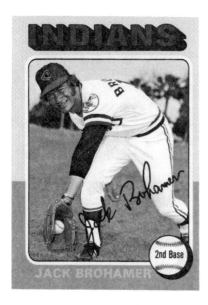

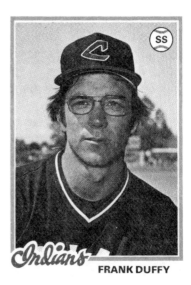

FRANK DUFFY

PAT DOBSON

ANDRE THORNTON

4
Owners
and
Presidents

1. How much did Charles Somers sell the Indians for on February 2, 1916?

2. How large of a bonus did "Sunny Jim" Dunn give his players after the Tribe won the 1920 World Series?

3. What did the players present Dunn with in honor of their Series victory?

4. How much did the syndicate headed by Alva Bradley purchase the Indians for on November 17, 1927?

5. Name the two legendary players Bradley tried to acquire after taking over as president and chief owner of the club. One played with

the New York Yankees, and the other was on the Boston Braves at the time.

6. How much did Bradley offer the Yankees for the player he coveted?

7. What is the title of Bill Veeck's autobiography?

8. Who was responsible for bringing Rocky Colavito back to the Tribe during his tenure as controlling owner of the franchise?

9. In what stadium did Vernon Stouffer plan to have the Indians play a minimum of 30 home games per season?

10. Who headed the syndicate that bought the club from Stouffer on March 22, 1972, and immediately put an end to the "twin-city concept"?

11. What Cleveland businessman and former Indians player made an attempt to buy the franchise from Stouffer before he sold to the syndicate headed by the man mentioned in the previous answer?

12. Who became the principal owner of the Indians on April 12, 1977?

13. During his reign as principal owner, the man mentioned in the previous question continuously searched for someone willing to purchase the club. One interested buyer was Donald Trump. Why did he refuse to sell the Indians to Trump?

14. How long did Richard and David Jacobs originally agree to keep the Indians in Cleveland for when they purchased the team?

15. Who was the first winner of the Cleveland Baseball Writers Man of the Year Award?

5

Hall of Famers

1. What year was the Baseball Hall of Fame formally opened to the public?

2. Where is the Hall located?

3. The original class was enshrined at the time of the museum's opening, but the election process had begun as early as January 1936. By the time of the Hall's dedication, there was a total of 26 inductees. Half of the men selected were chosen by 226 members of the Baseball Writers' Association of America. The other 13 were "old-timers", or those who played before 1900, voted in by a special veterans' committee. How many of the original 26 inductees wore a Cleveland uniform during their career?

4. How many from this class played for Cleveland?

5. Name those players.

6. How many from the initial class managed Cleveland?

7. Name those skippers.

8. Who was the next Indians player to be enshrined? In what year?

9. Name the next Cleveland pitcher to be inducted. What year was he enshrined?

10. Who was the second Indians infielder to be inducted? In what year was he enshrined?

11. What year was Earl Averill elected to the Hall?

12. This pitcher was on the Indians roster less than a year, but made 23 appearances in a Cleveland uniform. He was enshrined in 1994. Name him.

13. Name the former Major League umpire who once served as the Tribe's general manager (1927-35) and was elected to the Hall of Fame in 1973.

14. What year was Elmer Flick voted in?

15. Name the two teams Flick played on prior to his days as a Cleveland outfielder.

16. This pitcher was in the Major Leagues for only nine seasons, one less than the Hall requires for induction. But, an exception was made in this case, rightfully so, and he was enshrined in 1978. Who was he?

17. He played one season with the Indians (1955), but this leftfielder is often recognized as one of the games all-time best power hitters. He hit 369 homers during a 10 year career, 18 of which were for Cleveland. Most of his career was spent in Pittsburgh. Who was this player, and when was he enshrined?

18. In 1912, a "Nap Lajoie Day" was held in Cleveland to honor the great second baseman. Part of the celebration featured a nine-foot floral display of a horseshoe decorated with silver dollars. How many silver dollars were on the display?

19. How many hits did Lajoie amass during his career?

20. Who did not wear a tie during his induction ceremony in 1978?

21. Name the member who was inducted into the Hall of Fame as a manager only, despite the fact that he played catcher in the Majors for 19 seasons.

22. This pitcher was with the Detroit Tigers for 16-plus seasons before coming to Cleveland for a little over a year. He won two MVP awards with Detroit in 1944 and 1945 and is the only pitcher ever to win two in back-to-back years. Name him.

23. Name this one season-plus Cleveland pitcher, inducted in 1997, who won over 300 games and struck out over 3,000 batters during a 24-year career.

24. What year was Satchell Paige voted in?

25. This pitcher also won over 300 games and K'd more than 3,000 hitters. He played for eight Major League teams during 22 seasons. Who is he?

26. This 15 time .300 or better hitter played 97 games with the Indians in 1934. The other team he played for was the Washington Senators. Name him.

27. What year was Frank Robinson enshrined?

28. This Hall of Fame member holds the record for the best all-time strikeout ratio. He K'd once in every 62.6 at bats. Name this shortstop

who wore an Indians uniform for almost 10 full seasons and was inducted in 1977.

29. Name the Indians owner who was inducted in 1991.

30. During a 21-year career, this pitcher took the mound only for a brief time while playing for the Indians. Enshrined in 1985, he threw one of the best knuckle balls in the game. Who is he?

31. This pitcher, enshrined in 1972, was remembered for an aggressive, competitive nature. There were some who said he would brush back his own grandmother if she was at the plate with the game on the line. Who is he?

32. How many 20 or more victory seasons did the pitcher in the previous question post while on the Indians?

33. How many years did Cy Young pitch for the Cleveland Naps?

34. How many games did he win during his Major League career, which included a stint with the NL Cleveland Spiders 1890-98?

35. One final question that has nothing to do with Cleveland baseball, but everything to do with the Hall of Fame. Should Pete Rose be in the Hall of Fame?

6
<u>All-Stars</u>

1. In what year was the first modern All-Star game played? How many players were on each team, and what was the final score of the game?

2. How many Cleveland players were on the first All-Star roster and who were they?

3. None of the players in the previous question started for the American League that first year. Who was the first Indian to start an All-Star game, and what year was it?

4. Name the first Tribe pitcher to start an All-Star game. What year was it?

5. Who was the first Indians pitcher to win an All-Star game? What year was it?

6. Who was the second Cleveland pitcher to win an All-Star game and what year was it?

7. Name the first Indian to hit a home run in the All-Star game. What year was it?

8. What was the first year a Tribe player did not play in the All-Star game?

9. How many Indians were selected to the 1948 squad? Name them.

10. How many were selected in '54? Name them.

11. How many Indians were chosen in '95? Name these players.

12. Which Indians players started the '95 game?

13. How many times was Earl Averill selected to the team?

14. What year was Buddy Bell the only Indian to make the team?

15. How many times did Lou Boudreau play in the mid-summer classic?

16. How many seasons in a row was Larry Doby selected to the team while he played with Cleveland?

17. Name the Indians player who has been selected to the most All-Star games.

18. Who was the only Indians player to make the 1963 AL squad, but did not play? (Hint: he was a pitcher.)

19. Who was the only Cleveland player to be chosen to the '64 team, but also did not play?

20. How many times was Bob Lemon an All-Star?

21. Who was the only Tribe player to appear in the '69 mid-summer classic?

22. Who replaced Cleveland pitcher Ray Narleski in the 1956 game?

23. What year was second baseman Manny Trillo a starter in the All-Star game?

24. What year was the All-Star game first hosted by Cleveland?

25. Which Tribe players made the team that year, and what was the final score of the game?

26. What was the next year that the All-Star game was played in Cleveland? What was the outcome of the game?

27. First, name the player who hit two home runs in the game referred to in the last question, then name his two Tribe teammates who combined with him to knock in a total of eight runs.

28. What year was Cleveland the site of the All-Star game for a third time, and what was the final score?

29. On August 9, 1981, Cleveland Stadium was the site of the 52nd mid-summer classic. That game set an all-time attendance record for an All-Star game. What was the attendance total to the nearest thousand?

30. Name the Indians players who appeared in that game. What was the final score?

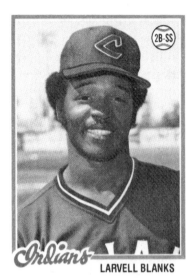

LARVELL BLANKS

RON PRUITT

JIM BIBBY

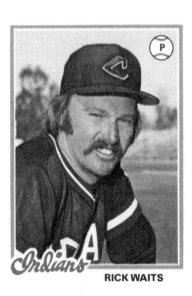

RICK WAITS

7
Nicknames
and
Real Names

1. Name the second baseman who, though his first name was Roberto, was called Bobby, and had the nickname of "Beto".

2. Why was Joe Azcue called "The Immortal Joe"?

3. What was Jim Bagby, Sr.'s nickname?

4. This top notch base stealer was adequately called "Deerfoot." Name him.

5. What was Buddy Bell's real name?

6. Who was known as "Strawberry Bill"?

7. What was Bert Blyleven's first and middle names?

8. What was George Burns's nickname? (No, not the comedian. The Tribe first baseman.) Also, is it true that his wife's name was Gracie? (Yes, like the comedian's wife and partner in humor.)

9. What was Chris Chambliss's real first name?

10. This player had one good season, giving false hopes to fans that the team found a "Super Joe" as he was called. Who had this nickname?

11. Although he never took the mound in clown attire, this pitcher who played in 26 games for Cleveland in 1959 was nicknamed "Bozo". What was his real name?

12. What was Rocky Colavito's actual first name?

13. What was Bo Diaz's real first name, and what was his nickname?

14. What was Bob Feller's nickname?

15. Known as Mike Garcia, this pitcher's nickname was "Big Bear". Actually, Mike was not his real first name. What was it?

16. What was Mudcat Grant's first name?

17. What were pitcher Mel Harder's two nicknames?

18. What was Toby Harrah's real name?

19. You've heard of "Crazy Legs" Hirsch, the football player, but what baseball player was known as "Piano Legs"? And why was he called this?

20. What was Sam McDowell's nickname?

21. What was Cal McLish's full name?

22. What was Minnie Minoso's full name?

23. What was Satchel Paige's first name?

24. This pitcher of four seasons-plus was nicknamed "Super Chief". Who was this?

25. What was Al Rosen's nickname?

26. Tris Speaker was often referred to as Spoke. First of all, what was Tris's full first name, and what was his other nickname?

27. Who had the nickname "Firebrand" because of his hot temper?

28. What was shortstop Terry Turner's nickname?

29. George Uhle was often referred to as "the smartest pitcher in the game", but he also batted .289 throughout a career that brought him up to the plate over 1,300 times. He holds several hitting records for pitchers, so it's easy to see why he earned his nickname. What was it?

30. This is a question most baseball buffs will think is easy, but don't worry if you don't know the answer. You will as soon as you look at the back of the book, and then you will be as smart as the rest of them (at least for this one question). What is Cy Young's full name, and why was he called "Cy"?

What were these players' nicknames?

31. Earl Averill

32. Stan Coveleski

33. Ray Fosse

34. James Seerey

35. Roy Weatherley

Whose nicknames were these?

36. Ding-Dong

37. The Human Rain Delay

38. Emu

39. Steam Engine In Boots

40. Rudy the Red-hot Rapper

8
<u>Uniform Numbers</u>

1. Name the two teams that were the first in professional baseball to wear numbers on the backs of their uniforms.

2. Where was the game played that featured the two teams that introduced this innovation? What year were numbers first worn on the backs of uniforms?

3. Other than having a shrine in Cooperstown, retiring a uniform number may be the highest honor for a player to achieve. The Cleveland Indians, like most Major League clubs, have had some players reach this level of immortality. How many Indians have had their numbers retired?

4. Who was the first Tribe player to have his number retired?

5. What number did he wear? What year was it retired?

6. Who was the second player to have his number retired by the Cleveland Indians?

7. What number did the player in the previous answer wear? What year was it retired?

8. This player had his number retired in 1975, which was also the year he was inducted into the Hall of Fame. Name him and his number.

9. In what year was Mel Harder's number retired? What number did he wear as a player for the Indians?

10. Name the player whose #14 was retired by the Indians in 1994.

11. Who wore #25 when he was on the team 1972-78?

12. What number did Joe Carter wear when he played for Cleveland?

13. Who wore #21 after he was acquired in 1965?

14. What number did Alvin Dark wear when he managed the Tribe?

15. What number did pitcher Mike Garcia wear?

16. What number did Orel Hershiser wear during the '95 championship season?

17. What number did Kenny Lofton wear during the '95 championship season?

18. What pitcher wore #36 during his stint with Cleveland 1972-75?

19. What number did Frank Robinson wear with the Indians?

20. What number did Sonny Siebert wear?

IV
LEGENDS

1
Shoelss Joe Jackson

Nowadays, the image we have of Shoeless Joe is whatever version Hollywood offers up, in films like *Eight Men Out* and *Field of Dreams*. An actor disappearing into a corn field, into some unknown realm, the producers would have us believe, where, at least there, he is with other immortals of the game.

How can we really imagine what kind of a ball player he was?

Joseph Jefferson Jackson was raised by impoverished parents in a small cotton-town in South Carolina. By the time he was 13, he was sent off to work at the mill, and never received much of an education. It has often been said that, due to the circumstances of his upbringing, he never developed a good sense of judgment. Some say he wasn't sophisticated enough to avoid the scandal that blackened an otherwise stellar career.

One thing he did have was a talent to play baseball.

A South Carolina newspaper's sports editor credited a fan with inventing the nickname, "Shoeless Joe", in 1908. It was at that time that Jackson played professionally for the Greenville Spinners of the Class D Carolina Association. One afternoon, Jackson, wearing a new pair of spikes, pitched part of a game, only to find out that it wasn't a good way to break in shoes. Blisters formed on his heels. The following day, playing in the town of Anderson, Jackson tried his best to play the outfield with his shoes on, but his feet were too sore. So, as the story goes, he made his final plate appearance in his socks, and hit a game winning home run. While he rounded the bases, an overzealous Anderson fan noticed he wasn't wearing his shoes, and hollered out, "You shoeless so-and-so."

Despite the derogatory meaning intended, the name stuck with him, and a legend was born.

Jackson came to Cleveland on July 30, 1910. Nobody in franchise history has bested his .375 batting average, accumulated during nearly five seasons with the club. Financial troubles forced the Indians to trade him to the White Sox on August 21, 1915. In the end, the deal proved to be a mistake for both Cleveland and Shoeless Joe.

Many of the people who saw him swing a bat called him the best natural hitter in the game. None other than Babe Ruth admitted to fashioning his stance after Jackson's. He had a lifetime batting average of .356, third only to Ty Cobb and Rogers Hornsby. Not once did he hit below .300 in a full major league season.

Jackson was the type of all-around player that today commands multi-millions of dollars. He had power, range, a glove like a tractor beam, and an arm nearly as precise as a weapon with a laser sight. During his Hall of Fame-type career, he swiped 202 bases, collected 1,172 hits, 307 doubles, 168 triples, 54 homers in the Dead Ball Era, and batted in 785 runs.

A funny thing happened on the way to Cooperstown. Shoeless Joe accepted a bribe. He conspired with seven of his White Sox teammates to throw the 1919 World Series. Now, though his ability on the field was never discredited, his integrity has been, and will be forever. Long after the last person to ever see him play has vanished.

Trivia Questions

1. The greatest player not in the Hall of Fame? Other than Pete Rose, probably. What was Jackson's highest season average, attained

in 1911, his first full year with Cleveland?

2. How many times did Jackson win the AL batting title?

3. How many times did he lead the league in hits?

4. How many triples did he hit in 1912 to pace the AL in that category?

5. What was his lowest batting average in a full season?

6. Name Shoeless Joe's first Major League team.

7. Jackson quit his first team on a couple of occasions, because his teammates mocked him for being illiterate. So he was traded to the Naps. Who did Cleveland give up in the deal?

8. Who were the three players Cleveland received from Chicago for Jackson in 1915?

9. How much cash did the Indians receive in the deal?

10. What was Jackson's annual salary while he played with the White Sox?

11. So, how much money did he admit to accepting from gamblers to lose the 1919 World Series?

12. How much was he promised?

13. All eight players involved in the scandal were expelled from the league in 1920. After being acquitted by a jury in a Chicago courtroom on August 2, 1921, baseball commissioner Kenesaw Mountain Landis decided not to re-admit the players, and they were banned from professional baseball for good. Fans of Shoeless Joe argue that he couldn't have thrown the Series. Jackson denied that he

did. He hit a home run, and had an impressive average during the eight games. What was his batting average in the 1919 World Series?

14. In the movie about the scandal, *Eight Men Out*, who played the Shoeless Joe Jackson character?

15. Who was the actor who portrayed him in *Field Of Dreams*?

2
Tris Speaker

His plaque in the Hall of Fame boasts: "the greatest center fielder of his day." It might be short-changing Tris Speaker a little by not adding: "one of the best hitters ever to step up to the plate."

For 22 seasons, pitchers feared his fluid, powerful cut. It was a sweet swing that connected 3,515 times for hits. 115 of those were home runs. That's not all Spoke was renowned for. He was a competent skipper who took the Indians to a World Series in 1920.

His defensive philosophy was to play shallow enough to take away the cheap hit, and let his speed carry him to those balls that seemed too deep to reach. Rarely did a ball go over his head. On occasion, he was in close enough to cover second base. This was especially effective during pick-off plays. Speaker would sneak up on a runner who held too big of a lead, field a pitcher's throw, and tag out the surprised runner before he could get back to the bag.

He didn't survive in the spacious confines of center field on speed alone. Speaker was an instinctive ball player. Through practice and trial-and-error, he learned to judge where a ball was heading the moment it was struck by a bat. Then his cat-quick reflexes enabled him to be striding toward the ball's destination long before it arrived.

Set backs abounded early in his career. His first Major League job came in 1907. He played in seven games with the Boston Red Sox where he only hit .158. Boston did not think he was worthy of a contract for the next season, so he tried out for the New York Giants. They weren't overly impressed either. All he could do was head back to the Red Sox training camp, and hope for a second chance.

Boston had a different idea. They gave Speaker to the Little Rock farm team in the Southern League. The motive behind this move was a simple one. Speaker was payment for the Red Sox use of Little Rock's field during spring training. That year he hit .350. By the end of the season, Boston bought back his rights.

With Speaker in center, Boston won the World Series in 1912 and 1915. Following four straight seasons in which his batting average declined from .383 in 1912 to .322 in 1915, Red Sox president Joe Lannin decided Spoke wasn't worth the pay increase he wanted. Never one to handle criticism very well, Speaker refused to play until a new deal was worked out.

It wasn't. Lannin announced that he would seek out a trade for his star centerfielder. Enter *Cleveland News* sports editor Ed Bang, who phoned Indians' GM Bob McRoy and informed him of Speaker's availability.

At first, Spoke spurned the Indians, saying that the team was going nowhere and the city wasn't an ideal place for professional baseball. Only after the Red Sox agreed to pay him a portion of the purchase price did the player recant.

April 8, 1916, the day of the transaction, was the beginning of a new era in Cleveland Indians baseball. One that lasted 10 years and provided fans and teammates with a lot of memories.

Trivia Questions

1. Where was Speaker born and in what year?

2. What year did he win the Chalmers Award, which happened to be an early version of the MVP Award?

3. How many doubles did he hit that year? How many stolen bases did he have?

4. What was his team leading batting average during the Red Sox 1912 World Series triumph?

5. What was Speaker's salary for the 1915 season?

6. Speaker expected a raise after the 1915 World Series. Joe Lannin mailed him his contract, but it wasn't what he had hoped for. How much did Lannin offer to pay him the following season?

7. Name the players Cleveland sent to Boston in the Speaker deal.

8. How much money did Cleveland pay to acquire him? How much money did Speaker receive from Boston as part of the deal that enabled them to trade him?

9. What was Spoke's highest single season batting average during his playing days with the Indians 1916-26?

10. What was his won-lost-tied record as manager of the Cleveland Indians?

11. Name the two teams he played for after the Indians.

12. Speaker holds the all-time Major League record for most assists by an outfielder. How many assists did he make during his career?

13. He also holds the record for most double plays ever by an outfielder. How many double plays did he make during his career?

14. How many putouts did he register during his career?

15. What is Tris Speaker's lifetime batting average?

SID MONGE

DUANE KUIPER

JIM KERN

RICO CARTY

3

Earl Averill

On opening day, 1929, Earl Averill did something we all dream about as youngsters. He stepped up to the plate for the first time in the big leagues and swung at an 0-2 pitch. The ball sailed over the fence, and he became only the third player to hit one out his first time up.

Now, not all of us make it to the Majors. Some of us go on to become doctors, architects, teachers or a thousand other necessary occupations. But Earl did make it, and he designed one heck of a career with a 5' 9½", 172- pound frame and a 44-ounce bat. (Others of us end up only *writing* about what ball players did.) He needed strong wrists to generate the type of bat speed that connected on 238 home runs during a 13-year stay in the league.

Those who aren't Tribe fans may remember him for breaking Dizzy Dean's toe by lining a pitch back at the mound in the 1937 All-Star game. That would be too bad. Averill was one of Cleveland's most beloved players. In 1938, the fans honored him with an "Earl Averill Day." One of the gifts the city faithful presented to him was a new Cadillac.

Born on May 21, 1903 in Snohomish, Washington, tragedy came early for Howard Earl Averill. His father died when he was 18 months

old. Playing baseball was pretty much a luxury for him during childhood, since he was needed on his family's farm.

After a couple of trials in semi-pro ball, Averill played with the San
Francisco Seals of the Pacific Coast League, where he was spotted by
Indians business manager Billy Evans. Averill, who had amassed
incredible numbers during his minor league days, including 36 home
runs and 173 RBIs in 189 games in 1928, was purchased by Cleveland
for a potentially risky sum of $50,000. Immediately, he showed that he
was more than just a hot prospect, winning the center field job before his
rookie season began. He established a then team record with 18 home
runs that year, and led AL outfielders with 388 putouts.

In over 10 seasons with the Tribe, he hit .322, and smashed 226 of
his career homers. Though he was considered to have a weak throwing
arm, as a result of an old high school injury, he was a top flight
defender. In short, he eased the pain of the fans who missed Tris
Speaker's play in center.

That is, until June 14, 1939, when he was traded to the Detroit
Tigers. Then all of Cleveland lamented the loss of the most explosive
hitter they'd had the pleasure to root for.

Trivia Questions

1. The day Billy Evans went to watch the San Francisco Seals play,
he had his sights set, not on Averill, but one of his teammates. Who
was this player the Indians were initially interested in?

2. Who was the pitcher Averill homered off of in his first time at bat
in the Majors?

3. What was Averill's batting average for his rookie season?

4. What did he do in a doubleheader on September 17, 1930 against
the Washington Senators?

5. What was his highest home run total in a season, and in what

years did he reach this number?

6. What team walked Averill five consecutive at-bats in a game played on August 29, 1932?

7. What season did he pace the American League with 232 hits and 15 triples?

8. Though its not up to par with Gehrig or Ripken's streaks, what was Averill's consecutive games played streak, beginning in 1931?

9. What was the freak accident that ended his streak?

10. What year did he participate in his only World Series?

11. How did he fare at the plate in that World Series?

12. Who was he traded to the Tigers for?

13. Name the team he ended his Major League career with in 1941.

14. Did Averill's son ever play baseball for the Indians?

15. During his induction speech at the 1975 Hall of Fame ceremonies, Averill stated his disagreement over the Hall's election process. He said: "I urge the changing of the rules before it is too late, so that all of those who deserve to be there while they are still living are so honored." Averill himself was selected for inclusion by a special veteran's committee, after fans and friends campaigned for years to have him inducted. What did he instruct his family to do if he was voted in after his death?

WAYNE GARLAND

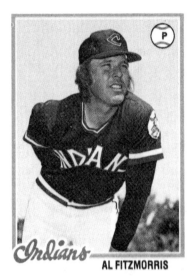

AL FITZMORRIS

INDIANS

INDIANS

4
Bob Feller

Bob Feller was the fastest pitcher of his day. Perhaps of all-time. It wasn't just the velocity of his speed ball that instilled fear in the hearts of the batters he faced. It was the way Feller delivered a pitch, turning his back to home plate, the ball hiding, then exploding forward as he uncoiled. Also, there was always one thing in the back of a hitter's mind. Though he was known as a strikeout artist, his 1,764 career base on balls meant that he didn't always control a pitch's destination with pinpoint accuracy.

Still, it would have been unreasonable to have expected him to. First of all, he was just 17 years old when he made his first Major League start on August 23, 1936. Over the years, he learned to keep his pitches in check better, resulting in only double digit figures in walks his final six seasons. And he never became notorious for bean balls, which tells us he didn't manufacture a wild streak despite the control problems. Second, wouldn't any arm that unleashed a projectile at nearly 100 miles per hour be prone to a near-miss now and then?

Actually, he may have thrown harder than that. Following World War II, the Army clocked his fastball at 98.6 miles an hour, but that was just about four years after he joined the Navy. Who knows how fast it moved when his arm was in game form, or in the shape it was at the beginning of his career.

From the beginning, it seemed that Robert William Feller was training to become a pitching phenom. Born November 3, 1918 on a farm in Van Meter, Iowa, his father began teaching him to throw at an early age. By the time he was six, he had developed a strong arm. To further condition his pitching arm, Feller threw baseballs against the side of his family's barn. His father set up a pitcher's mound and a home plate in the back yard, and the two of them would play catch whenever time allowed. As if that wasn't enough, the senior Feller built a ball diamond on the farm. He formed a team, with his son as the ace, and played other teams from the area.

From there it was on to semi-pro ball, where Feller was earning a paycheck of $30 per game. Also of note during this time were the five no-hitters he fired during his days at Van Meter High School. This brought him to the attention of Indians scout (and soon to be general manager) Cy Slapnicka.

The only problem with the pitcher was his age. Major League rules barred teams from contracting free agents still in high school. So, it was just a matter of keeping the kid a secret until he was old enough for the Indians to legally sign him.

Or was it?

Apparently not in the eyes of Slapnicka. Certain that it was only a short time before other organizations began showing interest in their find, Cleveland signed Feller in June of 1935, while he was 16. To cover it up, the franchise claimed he was an acquisition for the minor league team at Fargo-Moorehead of the Class D Northern League. He was soon transferred to New Orleans of the Class A Southern Association. In a move meant to keep their prize prospect under wraps, Feller was put on the "voluntary retired list" and never pitched in the minors.

Commissioner Kennesaw Mountain Landis found out about the Indians cover up. He ruled that, since Feller's signing opposed league policy, the kid was legally a free agent. The pitcher and his parents informed Landis of their desire to remain with Cleveland. Feller's father threatened to take Landis to court over the issue, and the commissioner reconsidered, allowing the boy to sign a new contract with the Indians.

Cleveland was fined $7,500. It was some of the best money the team ever spent.

By July 1936, Feller was ready for the big time. In his debut, an exhibition game against the St. Louis Cardinals, he struck out eight in three innings. He tied Dizzy Dean's single game record by striking out 17 Philadelphia Athletics in his fifth start. On the final day of the season, he established a new mark by fanning 18 Detroit Tigers.

Feller spent all or parts of 17 seasons with Cleveland. He won 266 games and struck out 2,581 batters in 3,827 innings. He also finished with 279 complete games and 44 shutouts. Those numbers would be higher if he hadn't missed more than three years to serve his country during the war.

Any way you look at it, Bob Feller, the once boy wonder on the mound of an Iowa farm, made it straight to big leagues and into Cleveland sports lore as the greatest pitcher the team ever had.

Trivia Questions

1. How much did Feller originally sign with the Indians for on July 25, 1936?

2. After agreeing to pitch for Cleveland, he continued playing semi-pro ball. Another Major League team "discovered" him while he played for Des Moines in a national tournament, and promptly offered him a $9,000 contract. Naturally, the Feller family had to turn down the offer. What team was this?

3. Who was the Indians opponent on the day Feller made his first Major League start?

4. How many batters did he strike out in his first start? What was the final score of the game?

5. What year did he win his first strikeout title?

6. How many times did he lead the league in strikeouts?

7. What was his highest strikeout total for one season, and in what year did he attain this mark?

8. What was his highest total for walks in a season? What year did he give up all these base on balls?

9. Name the battleship Feller was chief gunnery officer on during his service in World War II.

10. How many battle stars did he earn during his service?

11. How many times did he lead the American League in victories?

12. How many times did he win 20 or more games in a season?

13. How many no-hitters did he throw during his major league career? How many one-hitters?

14. What did fans nationwide vote Feller as for the game's Centennial Celebration in 1969?

15. In his own opinion, what was the toughest defeat Feller ever suffered?

5

Lou Boudreau

Popularity wise, there may never have been anyone in an Indians uniform equal to Lou Boudreau. Fielding wise, there can be no comparisons.

Louis Boudreau, Jr., was born on July 17, 1917, the son of a machinist-semi-pro ball player who taught him the ins and outs of the game. It is now legendary belief that Lou's father bought him an infielders glove when he was a child, and it lasted for a few seasons of Major League life before he needed to replace it. In high school, Boudreau showed remarkable athleticism and leadership ability, becoming the captain of the basketball team in his sophomore season. He earned all-state honors for three years in basketball, and led the team to a state title in 1933. He also starred on the varsity baseball squad.

At the University of Illinois he was captain of both the basketball and baseball teams. In 1938, he signed a contract with the Indians and made one pinch-hit appearance. Most of the season was spent at Cleveland's minor league affiliate, Cedar Rapids. The following year he played half the season with the Buffalo Bisons, and the other half in the Majors. With the Indians in 1940, he hit .295 and produced 101 RBIs.

For more than 10 seasons, he was the best shortstop in the game. At the time of his retirement, Boudreau had recorded the best career fielding percentage at his position. Not only did he have a vacuum for a glove, he had an uncanny instinct to pick up on a hitter's tendencies and seemingly knew where a ball was going before it leapt off the bat. He had a way of shrinking the vast area a shortstop covers. If runners did get on base, you could bet Boudreau would be anticipating their moves.

How much self-confidence did he have? Enough to apply for the Indians vacant manager's job at the end of the 1941 season at the age of 24. He wrote a letter to Indians owner Alva Bradley, expressing his interest in the position. He explained that his experience as captain of his college teams qualified him for the role. Despite second doubts, Boudreau sent the letter, and to his surprise was granted an interview. Even more surprising, on November 25, 1941, he was introduced as the 15th manager of the Cleveland Indians.

Though the Tribe didn't win a pennant his first six seasons as manager, fans kept Bill Veeck from trading Boudreau following a fourth place finish in '47. After the rumor of a trade was printed in the city newspapers, Veeck's office was flooded with letters of protest. Of 10,000 responses to a poll conducted by the *Cleveland News*, 90% voted that they wanted Boudreau to remain an Indian. Veeck responded by signing him to a two-year contract extension. You know the old saying: "The customer is always right." Well, its a good thing Veeck believed in that policy, because without Boudreau, Cleveland wouldn't have won the World Series in 1948.

He finished his career with a .295 batting average, 385 doubles and 789 RBIs. But it wasn't just the numbers. Boudreau was a hero to the city. Without him on the team from 1939-1950, Cleveland Stadium would have been a less popular place for fans to watch a ball game.

Trivia Questions

1. What high school did Boudreau attend?

2. What position did he play during his high school and college baseball days?

3. What Major League team declined to sign him out of high school, making it easier for him to decide to enroll at the University of Illinois?

4. How much did Boudreau sign with the Indians for in 1938?

5. The agreement he signed was to take effect after graduation. Why then did the Big Ten rule him ineligible to play?

6. Before he signed with Cleveland, what was Boudreau planning on doing after he graduated from the University of Illinois?

7. After he applied for the manager's position, the franchise's main shareholders took a vote on whether or not he'd get the job. He was initially turned down, 11-1. The lone holdout was able to convince the others of the logic behind such a move. He told them that a young manager, if he was surrounded by quality, veteran coaches, could be the spark the team was looking for. Who was the one shareholder who convinced the Indians Boudreau was their man?

8. What was the only year Boudreau led the AL in batting and what was his average for that season?

9. He also established a record for highest fielding percentage by a shortstop in a single season that year. What was his percentage?

10. He also set a record for most double plays by a shortstop that year. How many twin killings did he help turn?

11. What feat did Boudreau accomplish in the first game of a doubleheader against Boston on July 14, 1946?

12. What team did Veeck want to trade Boudreau to after the '47 season?

13. How many times did he lead the AL in doubles?

14. How many times did he lead the league in fielding percentage?

15. What was his lifetime fielding percentage?

16. Name the three Major League teams Boudreau managed after the Indians.

17. What was his lifetime record as a Major League manager?

18. One strategy Lou was famous for was first known as the "Boudreau shift", where he positioned all four of his infielders to the right of second base, leaving only the left fielder to patrol that side of the field. This tactic was used to defense one of baseball's all-time best pull hitters. Who was the player Boudreau defended this way?

19. Name the book he authored in 1949.

20. Name the Major League pitcher who one of Boudreau's daughters married.

6
Bob Lemon

First he was a third baseman, then Bob Lemon was converted to a centerfielder. The move made sense. He had a strong gun and the agility needed to track down fly balls, which he quickly demonstrated by robbing a White Sox hitter of extra bases in the '46 opener to save a 1-0 shutout by Bob Feller. Having belted 21 home runs at Baltimore of the Class AA International League in 1942, Lemon also showed he could use a bat.

Appearances, on the surface anyway, can be deceiving. He was actually a pitcher in a fielder's body. All that it took for manager Lou Boudreau to realize this was Lemon producing a measly .180 average after 55 games in 1946, his first year in the Majors. Then, after playing the role of bench warmer, Lemon threw batting practice one day. Boudreau was impressed and knew the Indians could use another strong arm on their pitching staff.

He began his pitching career in June of his rookie season, making five starts and a number of relief appearances. Over the years, he would win 207 games for Cleveland, while losing only 128. His career earned run average was a respectable 3.23, but at times, he was downright dominant.

Robert Granville Lemon was born in San Bernadino, California on

September 20, 1920. His playing days began as early as grade school. While playing shortstop at Woodrow Wilson High School in 1938, he caught the eye of an Indians scout and signed a contract. He worked his way up through the Tribe's farm system, posting numbers that indicated he would become a potent hitter. After a full season in the minors in '42, he spent three years in the Navy.

Most people learn their trade at an impressionable age, but not Bob. By the time of his switch to pitching, he was 26.

During his second season in the big leagues, the experiment became a success. He won 11 games, lost five and started a total of 15. The next season, the Indians championship year of '48, Lemon became a 20-game winner, while his ERA was near the top of the league.

He learned on the job, from game to game, developing one of baseball's all-time best sinkers. Instead of just dropping, the ball usually gave hitters the impression that it wanted to bury its face in the dirt at the very moment they swung. With a tough pitch in his repertoire, he led the AL in strikeouts in 1950 with 170. Naturally, his sinking fastball was not always the safest pitch to throw, and at times the strike zone was nowhere to be found. This resulted in his allowing a similar number of walks to strikeouts year in and year out.

After his playing career ended in 1958, Lemon focused his abilities on scouting and coaching. Ultimately, he became a successful Major League manager.

Trivia Questions

1. How much did the Indians sign Lemon for in 1938?

2. What did he buy with the bonus money he received in the deal?

3. In 1941 and 1942, Lemon played in 10 games with the Tribe. How many hits did he make in those plate appearances?

4. How many innings did he pitch while in the minors?

5. How many games did he play in the outfield for Cleveland in 1947?

6. How many times did he win 20 or more games in his Major League career?

7. How many seasons did he lead the American League in victories?

8. How many times did he lead the league in complete games?

9. How many times did he lead the AL in innings pitched?

10. How many games did he start during his Major League career?

11. How many innings did he pitch during his Major League career? How many strikeouts did he record?

12. What was Lemon's lifetime batting average?

13. How many times was he named *The Sporting News* Outstanding Pitcher?

14. Name the three Major League teams he managed.

15. What years was he voted Manager of the Year? Lemon also managed a team to a World Series title. What year was that?

V
MODERN STARS

1
Albert Belle

We can look at Albert Belle in two ways. Number one: he gave us a headache with his often publicized antics on and off the field. Number two: he was one heckuva ball player. Maybe the best player in the '90s, although White Sox fans would say Frank Thomas has that honor.

Let's discuss the latter.

After being drafted in the second round, following a successful college baseball career, Belle spent all of 1988 and part of '89 working his way up through the Indians farm chain. His first taste of Major League experience came in July of 1989. At that point, he was pacing the Eastern League with 20 home runs and 69 RBIs, so the Indians called on him to contribute some needed dynamite to their lineup. He didn't necessarily set the baseball world on fire. (Though his fuse was set to go off at any time—sorry, folks, I couldn't resist.) In 218 at bats, he hit .225, and deposited seven pitches into the bleachers. He started the next season with Cleveland, but his inability to adjust to big league pitching landed him in Colorado Springs (AAA) and Canton-Akron (AA). His breakthrough season came in '91, when he led the Tribe in homers and runs batted in. Two summers later, he was an All-Star, and by the end of the season, was the first Indian to lead the league in RBIs since Joe Carter did it in '86. His home run totals began equaling or eclipsing the numbers put up by the Game's best power hitters.

Nobody's numbers could compare to Belle's phenomenal '95 campaign of 50 home runs and 52 doubles, a .317 average and 126 RBIs. Still, his trouble in dealing with the press may have cost him the MVP Award. He finished second behind Boston's Mo Vaughn for the coveted honor. Instead, he was voted Major League Player of the Year by *Baseball Digest* and *The Sporting News.* He also won the Silver Slugger Award for a third straight year.

Following another power binge in '96, the Chicago White Sox made Belle the richest man in baseball. (At least until another "best player in the Game" comes along and signs a *bigger* contract.) He signed for a reported $11 million annually. After all the hassles he had with the White Sox over the years, I, for one, thought Belle *hated* Chicago. Well, money speaks louder than recollections, I guess. One thing should be remembered about Belle's departure though. Sure he took a big bat to the "Windy City." But along with his undershirts, socks and cleats, he also packed away a lot of problems. Which reminds me of a little joke I heard on the radio the other day: How many suitcases did Albert Belle take on his flight to Chicago? Answer: Seven. One for his personal belongings, and six for his temper.

Whoa, Albert. Don't blame me if you didn't think it was funny. I wouldn't make something like that up.

But I do have one question: Didn't anyone tell you that the media in Chicago is twice as obnoxious as it is in Cleveland?

Trivia Questions

1. Where was Belle born, and what is his full name?

2. What university did he play baseball for 1985-87?

3. How many home runs did he hit during the '86 and '87 seasons to establish school records for most hit out in a single season?

4. How many school offensive career records did he set while playing for the university?

5. Name the pitcher Belle got his first Major League hit off of in his first career at bat on July 15, 1989.

6. After being called up from the minors in '89, what position did Belle first play with the Indians?

7. How many home runs did he hit in 1991, his first full year with the Tribe?

8. How many RBIs did he collect in '93, to lead the American League in that category?

9. In '95, Belle became the first Major Leaguer since Stan Musial in 1948 to accomplish what feat?

10. How many votes did he lose the '95 AL MVP Award by?

2
Kenny Lofton

As is the case with any master thief, Kenny Lofton doesn't leave clues for his opponents to pick up on that enables them to catch him in the act. He never takes a more than honest lead, and he flinches about as often as a brick wall. When a pitcher glances over his shoulder, Kenny wears the expression of a politician. Nothing in his face tells you of his actual intentions, but you know you can't trust him.

You've heard the saying, "faster than a speeding bullet?" Well, the catcher's arm better be able to launch a ball that rapidly in order to catch him.

Not only does Lofton heist an extra 90 feet once in awhile, but he has also developed a sense of playing the warning track that is unparalleled in the game. If these were medieval times, they would want to cut off his hand for stealing baseballs from the fans sitting in the center field bleachers. Lofton attributes his defensive skill to speed, leaping ability, and great timing. There has to be a dash of divine blessing involved as well.

Born on May 31, 1967, in East Chicago, Indiana, Kenneth Lofton and his six siblings were raised by their grandmother. He credits her with teaching him the discipline and confidence needed to succeed in sports. In high school, he was a four-year starter on the baseball team, but it was at that time that he also became wrapped up in the area's traditional love for basketball. In fact, during most of his collegiate career, he dreamed about playing in the NBA. It wasn't until his junior year that Lofton rekindled an interest in his first passion. He made the varsity baseball team as a walk on, but ended up seeing little playing time. It didn't matter. The Houston Astros were impressed enough by his athleticism to draft him in 1988.

It was as much of a gamble for Lofton as it was for the Astros. He relinquished his hoop dreams in an effort to pursue a career in the Major Leagues. His first year at Class-A Auburn was nothing spectacular, as he compiled a .214 average, but he was promoted before the season ended. Two more years of minor league ball followed, and his average and fielding skills improved as he played more. In September of 1991, he was leading the Pacific Coast League in base hits (168) and posted a .331 average. The Astros called him up to the Big Show, but his stay only proved one thing to the Houston brain trust: Lofton needed more polishing.

John Hart agreed with that assessment. But the Tribe was in desperate need of a centerfielder, so Hart swung a deal. Lofton came to Cleveland on December 10, 1991, and went on to earn runner-up status in the Rookie of the Year balloting that following season. Before long, it became obvious that the Indians had the best centerfielder, and best base runner in the Game.

You might even say he stole that title.

Trivia Questions

1. What University did Lofton play basketball and baseball for?

2. In 1989, he started on the varsity basketball squad which was the number one ranked team in the country throughout most of the season. What position did Lofton play?

3. On the courts, he set a school record for steals in a season and in a career. He was also a finalist for an ESPN commentator's special year

end college basketball award. What award was this?

4. How many baseball games did he play during his junior season in college?

5. During his first Major League call-up with the Astros in '91, he played in 20 games. His batting average was .203 in 74 at bats. How many times did he strikeout while playing for Houston at the end of that season?

6. Name the player who beat out Lofton for AL Rookie of the Year honors in 1992.

7. How many bases did he steal his rookie season to lead the American League?

8. What year did he win his first Gold Glove?

9. What titles did Lofton win in a 1993 "Tools of the Trade" poll, in which Major League managers determined baseball's top players in a number of categories?

10. Name the two offensive categories Lofton led the AL in for the '95 season.

3
Charles Nagy

C harles Nagy always wanted to be a baseball player. Lucky for the Indians, he was dedicated enough to learn how to throw an assortment of good pitches.

Before he wore his first Tribe uniform, he traveled with Team USA for a 53-game schedule in the summer of '88 leading up to the Olympics. Then he made two appearances on the mound in Seoul, pitching a couple of scoreless innings and earning a save. Prior to that, he played college ball, high school and American Legion ball. As a youngster, he played in Little League and Babe Ruth.

You get the idea that when he was a baby, he turned down the rattle for a ball and glove and used his play pen as a backstop. Actually, Charles Harrison Nagy was born in Fairfield, Connecticut on May 5, 1967, and like all newborns, he probably had to be introduced to the game a little later in life. Back then, he most likely didn't realize he would pitch in the Olympics one day. Or in the World Series.

In June of '88, he was selected as the Indians second first round draft choice. The next season, his first year in pro ball, he racked up numerous honors, including Carolina League Pitcher of the Year. He was also named to *Baseball America's* Class A All-Star squad. By '91, he led Tribe pitchers with 10 victories in 33 starts. Unfortunately, 15 of his decisions were losses, but then again, the team lost a total of 105 games that year. So 15 suddenly doesn't seem that bad for a young pitcher. In '92, he won 17 out of 27 decisions. The next season was ruined by injury, but he became a stable starter during Cleveland's pennant runs in '94 and '95. Actually, during the Indians championship season, he showed he could be as dominant as any pitcher in the league, posting 16 victories. 12 of those came after mid-July.

Unfortunately, nothing Nagy could do prevented the Tribe from losing the '95 Series, or from bowing out in the first round of the '96 playoffs. But one thing remains a constant. As long as Nagy's on the mound, the Indians have a good shot at winning.

Trivia Questions

1. What high school did Nagy attend?

2. What three sports did he play in high school?

3. Name the college he played ball at.

4. What honors did he win for his pitching during college?

5. How high did the Indians draft Nagy in '88?

6. In his first season ('91), he led American League rookies in two pitching categories. What were they?

7. What feat did Nagy accomplish during the 1992 All-Star game?

8. What was his earned run average in '92?

9. His 16 wins in '95 tied him for the team lead with Orel Hershiser. He only had six losses. What was his ERA for that year?

10. How many victories did he post in '96? What was his ERA?

4
Manny Ramirez

By the time most people are still figuring out what they want to do in life, Manny Ramirez was cranking out home runs in the big leagues. He was one of baseball's top sluggers by his third season.

Born in Santo Domingo, Dominican Republic on May 30, 1972, it didn't take him long to realize that baseball could benefit him in many ways. By playing Pony League ball and American Legion ball during his adolescent years, he learned to be disciplined and mature. Those were two assets that helped him cope with his rapid rise to stardom.

Selected in the first round of the 1991 June draft, Ramirez spent a little over two seasons honing his skills in the minor leagues. In '91, he led the Appalachian League with 19 homers and 63 RBIs. He also hit .326, third highest average in the league. Those type of stats earned him recognition as Appalachian League Most Valuable Player. He was just as productive at AA and AAA levels, until being called up to Cleveland in September of '93.

He never looked back.

As the Indians regular rightfielder, he helped restore Cleveland to baseball prominence. Pitchers were more reluctant to pitch around Albert Belle and other Indians hitters knowing that Ramirez could just as easily deliver a crushing blow. He batted .269 his rookie season in

'94, with 17 home runs and 22 doubles. Even better in '95, he was a key part of the Tribe's offensive machine that routinely dismantled AL pitching. He hit .308 and increased his production in every offensive category. By duplicating those numbers in '96, he assured everyone involved with the franchise that he would be sending baseballs over the outfield wall for years to come.

Trivia Questions

1. What is Ramirez's full name?

2. What high school did he attend?

3. How many years did he earn all-city honors while playing high school baseball?

4. How high was he drafted by Cleveland in '91?

5. What award did he win after the '91 high school baseball season?

6. What honor did he win for the 1993 season while playing for AA Canton-Akron and AAA Charlotte?

7. Who did he get his first Major League home run off of on September 3, 1993?

8. Ramirez finished second in the 1994 American League Rookie of the Year balloting. Who beat him out for the honor?

9. In 1995, Ramirez became the first Tribe player since Hal Trosky in 1936 to accomplish what?

10. How many home runs did he hit in '96? How many runs did he bat in during that season?

VI
ODDS & ENDS

1
Trades
and
Acquisitions

1. What team was pitcher Johnny Allen acquired from on December 11, 1935?

2. What team was second baseman Bobby Avila traded to in 1958?

3. Name the two players Cleveland received for Jim Kern and Larvell Blanks in October of 1978.

4. Name the two players the Tribe received, along with Gene Bearden, when they traded Sherman Lollar and Ray Mack to the New York Yankees on December 20, 1946.

5. Who did Cleveland receive from Texas for Buddy Bell in 1978?

6. Who did Cleveland trade to the Toronto Blue Jays for Rico Carty in '76?

7. Name the players the Indians gave up to re-acquire Rocky Colavito on January 20, 1965.

8. What team did Cleveland trade pitcher Stan Coveleski to after the 1924 season?

9. Who were the two players the Indians received from the White Sox for Larry Doby on October 25, 1955?

10. What team was Lew Fonseca traded to for Willie Kamm in 1931?

11. Who did the Tribe trade to the Los Angeles Dodgers on April 3, 1974, for pitcher Bruce Ellingsen?

12. Name the two players and the cash amount Cleveland gave up to acquire Ralph Kiner from the Cubs on November 10, 1954.

13. Along with first baseman Preston Ward and pitcher Dick Tomanek, name the outfielder the Indians traded to the Kansas City Athletics for first baseman Vic Power and shortstop Woodie Held on June 15, 1958.

14. Who were the two players Cleveland acquired from the San Francisco Giants on November 29, 1971, for pitcher Sam McDowell?

15. What team did the Tribe acquire catcher Steve O'Neil from on August 20, 1911?

16. What team did Cleveland trade pitcher Jim Perry to in '63?

17. Name the player the Indians gave up to acquire Vada Pinson from the St. Louis Cardinals after the 1969 season.

18. Who did Cleveland acquire from the Washington Senators on June 13, 1917?

19. What team was Luis Tiant traded to in the winter of 1969?

20. Who were the players the Indians acquired from the White Sox on December 4, 1957, in exchange for Early Wynn?

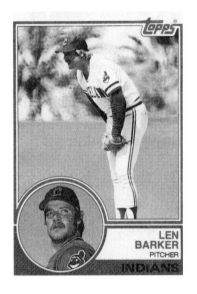

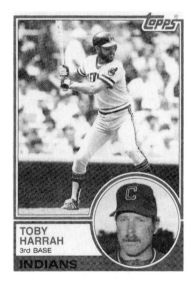

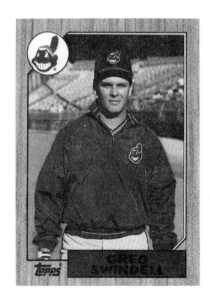

2
<u>Team Records</u>

1. Who has pitched the most games in Tribe history?

2. Who has pitched the most innings in Tribe history?

3. Name the pitcher who has the most career victories.

4. What pitcher has the most career losses?

5. Who holds the franchise record for most complete games?

6. Who holds the franchise record for most shutouts pitched?

7. Who holds the franchise record for most strikeouts in a career?

8. Of all the pitchers who have thrown over 1,000 innings in a Cleveland uniform, this hurler holds the team record for lowest career ERA. Who was he?

9. What pitcher holds the record for most wins in a season?

10. Who holds the record for lowest earned run average in a season?

11. Name the pitcher who holds the club record for most strikeouts in a season.

12. Bob Feller holds the team record for most complete games in a season, which he set in 1946. How many complete games did he pitch that year?

13. Feller also has the single season record for innings pitched. What is the record and when did he set it?

14. What team record did Stan Coveleski establish on May 14, 1918?

15. What dubious franchise record does Charles Baxter hold, which he set on April 28, 1901?

16. Who holds the team record for most games played in a career?

17. Joe Sewell holds the Indians record for most consecutive games played. How many games in a row did he play to set the record?

18. Name the player with the most career at bats with 6,037.

19. Who collected the most hits in team history?

20. This player hit 486 doubles during his Indians career to establish a club record. Who was he?

21. Albert Belle has the club record for most career home runs. How many did he hit while playing for the Indians?

22. Who holds the franchise record for most career RBIs with 1,085?

23. Who holds the record for most career runs scored with 1,154?

24. Who has stolen the most bases in club history?

25. Who holds the record for highest batting average in a season?

26. How about most hits in a season?

27. George Burns set a team record for most doubles in a season in 1926. How many two-baggers did he hit that year?

28. Who collected 162 RBIs in 1936 to establish a club record?

29. What club records did Johnny Burnett establish on July 10, 1932?

30. Name the Tribe player who holds the record for hitting the longest home run in Cleveland Stadium history on June 23, 1950.

3
Milestones & Awards

1. Name the first Cleveland player to lead the American League in batting.

2. Who was the first player in team history to lead the league in hits?

3. In 1915, Braggio Roth became the first Tribe hitter to pace the AL in homers. How many did he hit that year?

4. Name the first Cleveland player to lead the AL in RBIs for a season.

5. Who was the first Cleveland player to lead the AL in stolen bases when he swiped 45 in 1903?

6. Who was the first pitcher in franchise history to post a season league low earned run average?

7. Who became the team's first pitcher to win 20 or more games in a season?

8. What milestone did Cy Young achieve on July 19, 1910 versus the Washington Senators?

9. What milestone did Phil Niekro achieve on June 1, 1987?

10. What Cleveland player turned the first ever unassisted triple play on July 19, 1909?

11. What milestone did Bill Bradley reach on September 24, 1903?

12. What did Marty Kavanagh do on September 24, 1916?

13. When was the American League's first night game played? What team won the game?

14. Name the first Indian to earn Rookie of the Year honors.

15. Name the player who was the AL Rookie of the Year in 1980.

16. What Indians player was the first to win a Gold Glove Award in 1958?

17. Who was the first Indians shortstop to win a Gold Glove?

18. Who received *The Sporting News*' Silver Slugger Award in 1984?

19. Who received the Cy Young Award in 1972?

20. Who was named league MVP in 1953?

4
At the Movies

1. Name the Indians pitcher who plays himself during a baseball game scene in the movie "The Stratton Story", a film about White Sox hurler Monty Stratton. The film starred James Stewart.

2. This film, made in 1949, has the Cleveland Indians become a troubled young boy's "30 Godfathers." The movie, some of which was filmed at Cleveland Municipal Stadium, features several guest appearances by Indians ball players of the day, including Lou Boudreau, Bob Feller, Ken Keltner, Bob Lemon, Satchel Paige, and others, as well as owner Bill Veeck. Name the film.

3. Who portrays St. Louis Cardinals Hall of Fame pitcher Jesse Haines in the 1953 film, *The Winning Team*?

4. What role did Satchell Paige have in the 1959 Western, *The Wonderful Country*, which featured Robert Mitchum?

5. This utility infielder first became an actor on the soap opera *General Hospital* in the 1960s. He also made appearances in several movies. One of the better known films was *Marty*. Name him.

6. Name the Indians player who had a minor role in the 1974 film, *A Woman Under The Influence*.

7. What former Indian player portrayed a ball player in the 1976 Universal Studios picture, *The Bingo Long Traveling All Stars and Motor Kings*?

8. Name the actor who plays a retired Indians player in a movie called, *It's My Turn*, which came out in 1980.

9. A former Tribe player appears in the film mentioned in the previous question. Who was the player?

10. What is the name of the 1981 movie based on the life of Satchel Paige?

5

Broadcasters

1. We already know that Jack Graney became the first radio voice of the Indians. That was in 1946. Who was the team's first television announcer?

2. What was the TV station that first broadcast Indians games?

3. How many years did Tris Speaker broadcast Indians games on television along with Bob Neal?

4. How many years did Graney call Tribe games on the radio?

5. Who announced Indians games on TV for 10 seasons beginning in 1954?

6. In 1960, Lou Boudreau was a color commentator on radio for a Major League team. Early in the season he traded jobs with the team's manager. What team was it?

7. Who became a color commentator on Indians telecasts in 1964?

8. What year did Herb Score become the team's play-by-play man on radio?

9. Name the former Indians slugger who worked telecasts for the team in 1972, 1975 and 1976.

10. This former Indians center fielder became the color commentator for Cleveland's sportschannel affiliate in 1991. Name him.

6

Important Games

1. Who did the Bronchos play in Napolean Lajoie's Cleveland debut on June 4, 1902?

2. What team did the Cleveland Naps play on July 24, 1911?

3. What was the final score of the 1925 season opener against the St. Louis Browns?

4. How many singles did the Tribe collect against the Yankees on July 29, 1928? What was the final score of the game?

5. Name the Philadelphia Athletics pitcher who blanked the Indians, 1-0, in the first game played at Cleveland Stadium on July 31, 1932.

6. What was the significance of the game played on June 27, 1939?

7. Bob Feller made his return to baseball from World War II on August 24, 1945. The Indians played the Detroit Tigers. How many innings did Feller pitch that day? Did he win the game?

8. How did the Boston Red Sox clinch the American League pennant in a game played against Cleveland on September 13, 1946?

9. What happened on July 5, 1947?

10. What team did Rocky Colavito hit four home runs against on June 10, 1959, during an 11-8 Tribe win?

11. Name the four Indians who hit consecutive home runs in the sixth inning of the second game of a doubleheader played on July 31, 1963.

12. What was the significance of the game played on July 3, 1973?

13. What happened in the game played on April 8, 1975?

14. How many innings did the Indians and Twins play on August 31, 1993?

15. What was the significance of the game played on October 3, 1993, in which the Tribe lost to the White Sox, 4-0?

7
Final Exam

So you've read this book and are a bona-fide expert on the Cleveland Indians. Now you can call up all your friends and impress them with the volumes of information you have stashed away in your brain. They will gasp in awe, they will shower you with praise. By reading this book you have automatically become the life of the party, the "cool guy" everyone wants to be like. If used correctly, it may even do wonders for your love life.

Of course, your friends may be a little envious. If so, send them over to the nearest book store to pick up their own copy, so they can be part of the "in" crowd. Not that I'm inclined to offer a shameless plug on my own behalf. I wouldn't do such a thing. Writers just want to share the wealth of their vast knowledge. That's all. Money's not even in their vocabulary. Cash flow is though. And so is Big Bucks. A huge paycheck is something they think about from time to time.

Anyway, here it is. The ultimate sports quiz. The supreme brain teaser on the best baseball team in Cleveland history. The final test. The declaration if you will, of average-Joe fan, Super Genius. Forget about $E=mc^2$. You know the complicated steps it took for the Cleveland baseball team to get its name. I don't think Einstein even knew that.

Just a brief note on the exam that follows. These are general questions on the team, items of interest contained somewhere in the pages of this book. It will serve as a quick review of 10 essential facts every fan should know. If you pass with flying colors, consider yourself in the Hall of Fame for Tribe fans. If you bomb on it, don't tell anyone. You wouldn't want to risk becoming an outcast from society. Just try again, and use cheat notes if you have to.

Trivia Questions

1. What is considered to be the AL Cleveland franchise's first season in the Major Leagues?

2. What was the team's name that first season?

3. Who were the Cleveland Naps named after?

4. What year did the Cleveland baseball club become the Indians?

5. Who are the Cleveland Indians named in honor of?

6. Name the three stadiums or ball parks Cleveland has played their home games in over the years.

7. How many World Series titles have the Indians won? What years did the team win these championships?

8. What season did the Tribe win the most games in franchise history, and how many victories did the team get that year?

9. Who was traded to the Detroit Tigers on April 17, 1960?

10. Who purchased the Indians on December 11, 1986?

THE
ANSWERS

I - MEMORABLE SEASONS

1 - Before 1900
1. The Cleveland Forest Citys or The Forest City Club of Cleveland
2. Two (The Forest Citys disbanded during the 1872 season. That left Cleveland baseball-less until 1879.)
3. They traveled to Fort Wayne, Indiana to take on the Kekiongas.
4. Cleveland was defeated 2-0.
5. May 11, 1871
6. The Forest Citys were upset with home plate umpire, James L. Haynie, on what they considered to be one too many blown calls. Haynie was a well-known sportswriter for a Chicago newspaper. Fed up with what the Cleveland club viewed as favoritism, they protested by walking off the field.
7. 10 (seventh place)
8. Six wins, 15 losses
9. William Hollinger
10. Like the team six years before them, the new Cleveland club called themselves the Forest Citys. In 1882, the team was furnished with new, blue uniforms, so they changed the name to Blues.
11. 1884
12. 1880
13. Jim McCormick (During this time NL rules prohibited an overhand delivery. In other words, pitchers kept going and going, without needing to use Ben Gay.)
14. Richmond blanked the Forest Citys, 1-0, hurling the first ever perfect game in major league history.
15. He gave up the most runs in one game in major league history (35).
16. The American Association
17. 12
18. Boston Beaneaters
19. Boston won five games,

Cleveland none, and one contest ended in a tie.
20. The Temple Cup
21. a.) William C. Temple
 b.) four seasons
22. Cleveland played the Baltimore Orioles in 1895 and 1896. The Spiders won four games and lost one in '95, and were swept the following season, four games to zero.
23. $25,000
24. 20-134
25. The Infants

2 - The First Season
 1. April 24, 1901
 2. The Chicago White Sox
 3. The game was played in Chicago, at the 39th Street Grounds.
 4. Ollie Pickering (He flew out to center field.)
 5. Bill Hoffer
 6. Chicago won, 8-2
 7. Billy Hart
 8. Milwaukee Brewers (Not the team from today.)
 9. Cleveland won, 4-3.
10. Hoffer
11. James R. McAleer
12. St. Louis Browns
13. Three
14. Nine (The score was 14-3.)
15. John F. Kilfoyl
16. The original AL Baltimore Orioles
17. 55-82 (Seventh place)
18. Earl Moore
19. Pete Dowling

20. Left fielder Jack McCarthy

3 - Title Hopes (1908)
 1. Ty Cobb
 2. Right fielder Elmer Flick
 3. Jennings told Somers that Cobb was a disruption to the team and could not get along with his teammates, so it was in the Tigers best interest to deal him. Somers turned down the offer, because Flick was "much nicer to have on the team."
 4. Every batter in the Naps lineup collected a hit and scored a run that inning.
 5. Bob "Dusty" Rhoades
 6. Two dollars
 7. Addie Joss
 8. Addie Joss
 9. Chicago White Sox and Detroit Tigers
10. a.) Detroit Tigers
 b.) Cleveland ended up a half game behind Detroit, and Chicago 1½ games out. The reason for the half-game difference was that the Tigers had a game rained out in August, and the AL did not require rain outs to be made up.

4 - Good-bye, Nap (1914)
 1. 51
 2. 102
 3. Joe Birmingham
 4. Two (June 30 and July 1)
 5. 48½ games
 6. Babe Ruth
 7. He collected his 3,000th hit on September 27.

8. .258
9. Naps owner Charles Somers, who owned the former Toledo franchise
10. 185,997

5 - Pennant Fever
(1921 and 1926)
1921
1. Bill Wambsganss
2. Steve O' Neill
3. 23
4. Elmer Smith
5. Tris Speaker
6. George Uhle
7. The Polo Grounds in New York
8. Unfortunately, the Yankees won three games and finished 4½ ahead of the second place Indians.
9. Babe Ruth
10. .308

1926
1. Emil "Dutch" Levsen
2. 33
3. 64
4. George Uhle
5. NY Yankees
6. Five
7. Four (It left them three games back.)
8. Yankees by three games
9. Hubert "Dutch" Leonard
10. Landis deliberated the case for nearly two months before declaring his verdict. He said: "These players have not been, nor are they now found guilty of fixing a ball game. By no decent system of justice could such a finding be made." Landis acquitted all four

players of any wrong doing on January 27, 1927.

6 - Mutiny On The Diamond
(1940)
1. He became the first major league pitcher to throw a no-hitter on opening day.
2. Jeff Heath scored off Rollie Helmsley's fourth inning triple.
3. 27 wins, 261 K's
4. Oscar Vitt (Bradley later admitted that he made a mistake by not firing Vitt right away. Instead, he waited until after the season.)
5. Former Tribe catcher Luke Sewell who was a coach for the team in 1940.
6. The Cleveland Crybabies
7. Jeff Heath, Roy Weatherly, Hank Helf and Oscar Grimes
8. Roy Weatherly (He earned the bonus.)
9. Floyd Giebell (It was his last major league victory.)
10. 89 (65 losses)

7 - The Day Cleveland Cried
(1960)
1. Cleveland manager Joe Gordon
2. Two
3. Detroit Tigers
4. Harvey Kuenn
5. One (Just 1960)
6. Kuenn led the team with a .308 average.
7. Right field
8. 42
9. 129
10. Detroit Tigers (Tigers won, 4-2.)
11. The Indians dealt first baseman

Norm Cash for third baseman Steve Demeter.

12. Lane and Tiger GM Bill Dewitt pulled off the only trade in Major League history that involved two managers. That's right. Gordon was traded for Tigers manager Jimmy Dykes.

13. Joyner "Jo Jo" White

14. Kansas City Athletics

15. 51 total

16. San Francisco Giants

17. The Angels selected Gene Leek, Ken Aspromonte and Red Wilson. Washington chose Jim King, Marty Keough, Carl Mathias and Johnny Klippstein.

18. 1960 - 35
1961 - 45
1962 - 37
1963 - 22

19. 1965 (January 20th)

20. The Kansas City Athletics

8 - Happy Hour At the Stadium(1974)

1. Rocky Colavito
2. Larry Doby
3. Chris Chambliss
4. Frank Robinson
5. 586
6. One dollar
7. Gaylord Perry (21 wins) and his older brother Jim (17)
8. 10 cents
9. Texas Rangers
10. In the later innings, the fans, drinking heavily that night, got out of hand. They continuously ran onto the field, delaying the game's

progress. In the bottom of the ninth inning, the Indians scored two runs to knot up the score, 5-5. With two outs and the winning run ninety feet away, hundreds of spectators ran on the field again for a premature celebration, and to attack some of the Texas players. Coaches and players were forced to battle their way to the clubhouse to wait out the delay. After 15 minutes of trying to restore order, umpire Nestor Chylak forfeited the game to the Rangers. The official score of the game then, as it is with any forfeit in baseball, was 9-0.

9 - New Power Surge (1986)

1. 84 wins, 78 losses
2. .284
3. 831
4. Joe Carter
5. Four
6. Tony Bernazard (.301), Joe Carter (.302), Julio Franco (.306) and Pat Tabler (.326)
7. Tom Candiotti
8. Candiotti
9. Brett Butler
10. Greg Swindell

II - WORLD SERIES

1 - 1920

1. 98
2. 56
3. They were the eight players indicted by a Cook County, Illinois grand jury for the infamous "Black

Sox" scandal, in which they were bribed into throwing the 1919 World Series against the Cincinnati Reds.

4. .296
5. Harry Lunte
6. Joe Sewell
7. Jim Bagby, Sr.
8. Stan Coveleski
9. 93-61
10. a.) Seven
 b.) Cleveland won five games
11. Coveleski (Cleveland won, 3-1.)
12. Burleigh Grimes - Game Two (won by Brooklyn, 3-0); Sherrod Smith - Game Three (also won by Brooklyn, 2-1)
13. He hit a grand slam.
14. He turned an unassisted triple play.
15. Jim Bagby (It was a three-run shot in the fourth inning.)
16. Walter "Duster" Mails
17. Coveleski
18. October 12, Columbus Day
19. $4,204
20. Since they were defending their title the following year, "World Champions" was printed across the front of the players' uniforms.

2 - 1948
1. Hank Greenberg
2. Bob Lemon
3. Satchel Paige
4. Kansas City Monarchs
5. Boudreau (He didn't hit the pitches with much authority, so Paige earned a spot on the roster.)
6. a.) Seven
b.) Six (One loss)
c.) Two

d.) 2.48
7. Boston Red Sox at Fenway Park
8. Gene Bearden
9. Veeck said: "We did not win the pennant in 1948. We won it on November 25, 1947, the day I rehired Lou Boudreau."
10. Bearden (20 wins) and Bob Lemon (20 wins)
11. Second baseman Joe Gordon
12. Boston Braves
13. Cleveland started ace Bob Feller and Boston started Johnny Sain, their top pitcher as well. Boston won, 1-0.
14. Feller had thrown the ball to shortstop Boudreau in an effort to pick off base runner Phil Masi at second base. Boudreau caught the ball and applied the tag as Masi dived back to the bag head first. Stewart signaled safe, insisting Boudreau had attempted the tag too high, allowing the runner to slide safely back before Lou's glove touched him. Photographs disputed the call, showing the tag being applied before the runner's hands touched the bag. One out later, Tommy Holmes singled, and Masi scored the only run of the game.
15. Lemon won Game Two, 4-1, and Bearden pitched a 2-0 shutout in the third game.
16. The two heroes were pitcher Steve Gromek, who hurled a complete game seven hitter, and outfielder Larry Doby, who hit a home run in the first inning that was

the eventual game winning run.

17. 86, 288

18. Bob Elliot

19. Boudreau brought in Gene Bearden. He gave up a sacrifice fly to the first hitter he faced, trimming the lead to two runs, as the runner on third scored. The next batter, Tommy Holmes, doubled in a run to make it, 4-3. Mike McCormick then grounded out to Bearden to end the threat. Cleveland held on in the ninth for the victory, and a four games to two World Series triumph.

20. Doby, Joe Gordon, catcher Jim Hegan and left fielder Dale Mitchell

3 - 1954

1. 111 (They dropped 43.)

2. Bobby Avila

3. He played second base for 10 seasons (1949-58).

4. 32 homers and 126 RBIs

5. Bob Feller, Mike Garcia, Art Houtteman, Bob Lemon and Early Wynn

6. a.) Wynn

b.) Lemon

7. 23

8. 77

9. Home runs (156)

10. The Yanks became the fourth team to ever reach 100 victories in a season, but not win the pennant. They were 103-51, eight games behind Cleveland.

11. Al Rosen played 10 seasons in Cleveland (1947-56)

12. Vic Wertz

13. He printed "We're In" on the top

of his bald head. The message was written with lipstick.

14. The New York Giants

15. 97-57

16. Wertz

17. Dusty Rhodes hit one of the shortest homers in World Series history. It was only 258 feet down the right field line.

18. Rhodes

19. Wertz

20. Unfortunately, the Giants swept Cleveland in four games, by scores of 5-2, 3-1, 6-2, and 7-4.

4 - 1995

1. Eddie Murray (.323), Albert Belle (.317), Jim Thome (.314), Carlos Baerga (.314), Kenny Lofton (.310), Manny Ramirez (.308) and Sandy Alomar, Jr. (.300)

2. 17

3. 54

4. Two

5. Chad Curtis

6. Baltimore Orioles

7. Jim Thome

8. No. Not this time.

9. Zero

10. Bob Wolcott

11. Kenny Lofton

12. Orel Hershiser won Game Two and Five.

13. 95

14. Javy Lopez

15. Eddie Murray

16. Game One: 3-2 Atlanta
Game Two: 4-3 Atlanta
Game Three: 7-6 Cleveland
Game Four: 5-2 Atlanta

Game Five: 5-4 Cleveland
Game Six: 1-0 Atlanta
17. Cleveland started Hershiser and Atlanta started Tom Glavine.
18. Tony Pena
19. David Justice
20. Jim Poole

III - PERSONNEL DEPARTMENT

1 - Position Players
1. 17
2. Milwaukee and Atlanta Braves, New York Mets, Chicago White Sox, California Angels, New York Yankees and Texas Rangers
3. Alan Ashby
4. The Mexican League
5. a.) Carlos Baerga
 b.) Seventh inning
6. Harry Bay
7. Buddy Bell
8. a.) Ray Boone
 b.) His son's name is Bob and his gandson's name is Brett.
9. Bill Bradley
10. Nine (1963-71)
11. George Burns
12. a.) Detroit Tigers
 b.) Seven (1920-21, 1924-28)
13. 1984
14. Joe Carter
15. Carty signed with 10 teams. After sorting through the contracts, the Milwaukee Braves were the winners in the "Rico Carty Sweepstakes."
16. Rocky Colavito
17. Vic Davallilo
18. Four (He did not name the players.)
19. The Newark Eagles of the Negro League
20. Frank Duffy
21. Luke Easter
22. Lew Fonseca
23. 1983
24. Tito Francona
25. Oscar Gamble
26. Jack Graney
27. Jack Graney
28. Jeff Heath
29. 293
30. Jim Hegan
31. Oakland Athletics
32. Johnny Hodapp
33. Dick Howser
34. Brook Jacoby
35. He started a triple play in both games.
36. 14 (1919-1932)
37. He was suspended by Tribe manager Walter Johnson for being —in Johnson's opinion—a leader in a movement against the manager. Therefore, he was considered to be detrimental to the well being of the team. Owner Alva Bradley refused to get involved in the disciplinary aspects of the players, but instead named Kamm a team scout. His playing days ended there.
38. Ken Keltner
39. He hit the only home run of his major league career that day.
40. Ray Mack
41. Shortstop
42. 314
43. Dale Mitchell
44. Ozzie Smith
45. O'Dea was hit in the right eye

by a foul pitch during spring training batting practice. He was permanently blinded in that eye. After several operations, he played two seasons with the team ('44 and '45) then retired.

46. Steve O' Neill (He became the full-time starter in 1915, until he was traded.)

47. Ollie Pickering

48. 34

49. He played mostly first base, but also played a few games at second short and third.

50. a.) Frank Pytlak and his back-up Hank Helf

b.) The record was achieved when Pytlak and Helf each caught a ball that was dropped from the top of the Terminal Tower, located in Cleveland's Public Square. The total height of the drop was 708 feet.

51. .285

52. 192

53. 43

54. Chico believed in the supernatural. He had a fear of ghosts, so he kept the lights on when he went to bed, hoping it would prevent him from seeing any.

55. Pat Seerey

56. 12½ (mid-1921-32 and 1939)

57. Al Smith

58. Cory Snyder

59. He became the first top major league player to jump to the Federal League, which was viewed as an outlaw organization.

60. Eight (1904-11)

61. Jim Thome

62. 216

63. Chicago White Sox

64. 15 (1904-1918)

65. 9

66. Joe Vosmik

67. a.) outfield

b.) Six-plus seasons (some of 1930 to 1936)

68. 329

69. 1906

70. The Indians committed 87 errors during the strike-shortened season of 1981.

2 - Pitchers

1. Umpire Bill McGowan told Allen to change his under shirt, or cut off the torn right sleeve which Red Sox batters complained was distracting them. Instead of complying, Allen left the field. In the clubhouse, manager Oscar Vitt ordered him to follow the umpire's demand. Allen refused and did not play the rest of the game. As a result, he was fined $250.

2. Jim Bagby, Jr.

3. Jim Bagby, Sr. and Jim Bagby, Jr.

4. Len Barker

5. Gary Bell

6. Bill Bernhard won 23 games that season.

7. Bert Blyleven

8. Sometimes they say the easiest play is the hardest, especially when greatness is waiting there if you succeed. Bosman himself fielded a come back to the mound, turned

and threw the ball to the ball boy sitting along the sidelines probably. The throw was well over first baseman Tom McCraw's reach. That was the only base runner Bosman allowed and he settled for a no-hitter.

9. Ernie Camacho
10. Tom Candiotti
11. Russ Christopher
12. a.) no hits
b.) three walks
c.) no runs
13. Philadelphia Phillies
14. a.) 87
b.) 40 (32 losses)
15. 23
16. Wesley Ferrell
17. Four
18. Not including his one appearance in 1948, Garcia was a Tribe pitcher for eleven seasons from 1949-59. He won 142 games while losing 96.
19. Wayne Garland
20. Wayne Garland threw 21 complete games in 1977.
21. 23
22. Gromek injured his left shoulder, which he feared would limit his hitting ability.
23. One win, 13 defeats
24. He told Johnny that he sang hymns to himself.
25. Otto Hess
26. Charlie Hickman
27. 15 (1926-40)
28. 1927
29. 30
30. He deliberately forced the trade by breaking the long-standing Reds clubhouse rule that forbids facial hair. Kern sported a beard until the move was made.
31. Dennis Martinez
32. Sam McDowell
33. He gave up four home runs in one inning. It was the sixth inning.
34. Jose Mesa
35. Jake Miller
36. Sid Monge
37. Chicago White Sox
38. Chad Ogea
39. Allie Reynolds
40. St. Louis Cardinals
41. $60,000
42. Joe Shaute (He struck out Ruth 33 times.)
43. Paul Shuey
44. First base and outfield
45. Al Smith (He's not the same Al Smith who played outfield and third base for the Indians in the 50s.)
46. 35
47. Bobby Avila (He signed Tiant to pitch for the ball club he owned which was called the Mexico City Tigers.)
48. The team was called the Cleveland Standard Parts.
49. Bob Feller (righty) and Vean Gregg (lefty)
50. Nine times (1901-09)

3 - Managers
1. James McAleer
2. William R. Amour
3. 377 (309 losses)
4. Lou Boudreau
5. Boudreau
6. Chicago White Sox
7. Greenberg wanted to hire Leo

Durocher, who, at the time, worked for NBC-TV. Durocher wanted a hefty salary. Too hefty for Greenberg's liking, so the Indians hired Kerby Farrell instead.

8. Harder won all three games in which he served as an interim manager. He managed one game in 1961, and a twin bill in '62.

9. Birdie Tebbetts

10. Alvin Dark

11. Ken Aspromonte

12. Frank Robinson (1961 with Cincinnati and 1966 with Baltimore)

13. Jeff Torborg (He was hired by Robinson to coach for Cleveland. Torborg did not want to replace Robinson without his blessing, but Robinson told him if he didn't take it someone else would. Torborg managed the team from 1977-'79.)

14. John McNamara (1990-91), Doc Edwards (1987-89), Pat Corrales (1983-87)

15. .290

16. First base

17. Lou Boudreau (nine seasons)

18. Frank Robinson

19. Eight

20. 1) James McAleer
2) Nap Lajoie
3) George Stovall
4) Harry Davis
5) Joe Birmingham
6) Tris Speaker
7) Lou Boudreau
8) Frank Robinson

4 - Owners and Presidents

1. $500,000

2. The players each received bonuses equivalent to 10 days pay.

3. Diamond cuff links

4. $1 million

5. The players were Lou Gehrig and Rogers Hornsby

6. $250,000 plus George Stovall

7. *Veeck - As In Wreck*

8. Gabe Paul

9. The Louisiana Superdome in New Orleans

10. Nick Miletti

11. George Steinbrenner and Al Rosen

12. Alva T. "Ted" Bonda

13. Bonda did not want to sell the franchise without a guarantee that the buyer would keep the Indians in Cleveland. He wisely felt that Donald could not make such a promise.

14. In order to buy the Indians, the Jacobs brothers had to promise to keep the team in Cleveland for at least five years.

15. Bill Veeck

5 - Hall of Famers

1. 1939

2. Cooperstown, New York

3. Four

4. Three

5. Nap Lajoie, Cy Young and Tris Speaker

6. Three

7. Nap Lajoie, Tris Speaker and Walter Johnson

8. Bob Feller

9. Stan Coveleski in 1969

10. a.) Lou Boudreau

b.) 1970
11. 1975
12. Steve Carlton
13. Billy Evans
14. 1963
15. He first played with the Philadelphia Phillies of the National League, then the Philadelphia Athletics of the AL for 11 games before being sold to Cleveland.
16. Addie Joss
17. Ralph Kiner in 1975
18. 1,009 silver dollars
19. 3,242
20. Bob Lemon
21. Al Lopez
22. Hal Newhouser
23. Phil Niekro
24. 1971
25. Gaylord Perry
26. Sam Rice
27. 1982
28. Joe Sewell
29. Bill Veeck
30. Hoyt Wilhelm
31. Early Wynn
32. Four (1951, 1952, 1954 and 1956)
33. Nearly three seasons (He pitched for the Naps from 1909-11, but was released on August 15, 1911.)
34. 511
35. Of course. Look at the numbers. Hopefully someday a commissioner will make the proper decision and restore Rose's eligibilty. Besides, does gambling —even if a player bets on his own team—inhibit his performance any more than drugs do? Rose means

more to the game than his banishment does to the upholding of justice.

6 - All-Stars
1. The inaugural mid-summer classic was played on July 6, 1933 at Comiskey Park in Chicago. Each squad consisted of 18 players. In that game, the American League defeated the Nationals, 4-2.
2. a.) Three
b.) Earl Averill, Wes Ferrell and Oral Hildebrand
3. Joe Vosmik in 1935
4. Bob Feller in 1941
5. Mel Harder in 1934
6. Feller in 1946
7. Lou Boudreau in 1942
8. 1945 (No game was played.)
9. a.) Five
b.) Boudreau, Feller, Joe Gordon, Ken Keltner and Bob Lemon
10. a.) Five
b.) Bobby Avila, Larry Doby, Mike Garcia, Bob Lemon and Al Rosen
11. a.) Six
b.) Carlos Baerga, Albert Belle, Kenny Lofton, Dennis Martinez, Jose Mesa and Manny Ramirez
12. Baerga and Belle
13. a.) Six
b.) Three
14. 1973
15. Five (He was selected two other times, but did not play in the game. Lou was also chosen in 1945, but there was no game played that year.)
16. Seven (1949-55)

17. Feller (eight times)
18. Mudcat Grant
19. Jack Kralick, pitcher
20. Seven
21. Pitcher Sam McDowell
22. Herb Score
23. 1983
24. 1935 (July 8)
25. a.) Mel Harder, Joe Vosmik and Earl Averill, who did not play due to injury
 b.) The AL won, 4-1.
26. a.) 1954 (July 13)
 b.) AL -11, NL -9
27. Al Rosen hit the two homers, while he, Bobby Avila and Larry Doby paced the AL team with 8 RBIs.
28. The game, won by the NL, 5-3, was played in 1963 (July 9).
29. 72,086
30. a.) Len Barker, pitcher and Bo Diaz, catcher
 b.) the NL won, 5-4

7 - Nicknames and Real Names
1. Bobby Avila
2. A teammate dubbed Azcue "Immortal" after the catcher fell asleep in the bull pen during his first game with Cleveland on May 25, 1963. The night before was spent catching a flight so he could join the team he had been traded to. The Indians starting catcher, John Romano, broke his right hand after being hit by a foul pitch, so Azcue was awakened and rushed into the lineup. He provided the winning hit later in the game.

Azcue contributed many clutch hits throughout the rest of the season, and the nickname stuck.
 3. Sarge
 4. Harry Bay
 5. Gus Bell
 6. Bill Bernhard
 7. Rik Aalbert
 8. a.) Tioga George
 b.) Yeah right. I put that in for the sake of humor.
 9. Carroll
10. Joe Charboneau
11. Al Cicotte (Maybe it was his pitching that earned the nickname.)
12. Rocco
13. First name - Baudilio; Nickname - The Cannon
14. Rapid Robert
15. Edward
16. James
17. Chief and Wimpy
18. Colbert Dale Harrah
19. a.) Charles Hickman
 b.) Because he had thick, muscular legs.
20. Sudden Sam
21. Calvin Coolidge Julius Caesar Tuskahoma McLish
22. Saturnino Orestes Armas Minoso
23. Leroy
24. Allie Reynolds
25. Flip
26. Tristram; The gray Eagle
27. George Stovall
28. Cotton
29. The Bull
30. His full name is Denton True Young, but he was called Cy after

the first catcher who played with him said his fastball resembled a "cyclone."

31. Rock, or The Earl of Snohomish
32. Covey
33. Mule
34. Fat Pat
35. Stormy, or Little Thunder
36. Gary Bell
37. Mike Hargrove
38. Jim Kern
39. Earl Moore
40. Rudy Regalado

8 - Uniform Numbers

1. Cleveland Indians and New York Yankees
2. The game in which Cleveland and New York first wore numbers was played at League Park in 1929, on May 13 to be exact.
3. Five
4. Bob Feller
5. Feller wore number 19, which was retired in 1957.
6. Lou Boudreau
7. a.) Number 5
b.) 1970
8. Earl Averill, who wore number 3.
9. a.) 1990
b.) Number 18
10. Larry Doby
11. Buddy Bell
12. 30
13. Rocky Colavito (Okay. So he was actually re-acquired in '65. I had to make it a little difficult.)
14. 5
15. 25
16. 55

17. 7
18. Gaylord Perry
19. 20
20. 42

IV - LEGENDS

1 - Shoeless Joe Jackson

1. Shoeless Joe batted .408 for the year. Amazingly, it was not the highest average in 1911. Ty Cobb hit .420 to win the batting crown.
2. None (Not even when he hit .395 in 1912, or .373 in '13 and .392 in 1920, the year he was banned from the game for life.)
3. Twice (1912 and 1913)
4. 26
5. He hit a career low .301 for Chicago in 1917.
6. Philadelphia Athletics
7. Bris Lord (Never heard of him, huh?)
8. Outfielders Larry Chappell and Bobby Roth, and pitcher Ed Klepfer
9. $31,500
10. $8,000
11. $5,000
12. $20,000
13. .375
14. D.B. Sweeney
15. Ray Liotta

2 - Tris Speaker

1. He was born in Hubbard, Texas in 1888 (April 4).
2. 1912
3. 53 doubles, 52 stolen bases
4. He hit .300 for the Series.
5. $9,000

6. Lannin expected him to play at the same rate of his previous contract.

7. Pitcher "Sad Sam" Jones and third baseman Fred Thomas

8. a.) Cleveland paid $50,000 b.) Spoke was paid $10,000 by his former team.

9. He hit .389 in 1925.

10. 617 wins, 520 losses and two ties

11. He finished his playing career with one season each on the Washington Senators and the Philadelphia Athletics.

12. 448

13. 139

14. 6,787 (An all-time American League record.)

15. .345

3 - Earl Averill

1. Outfielder Roy Johnson (The Tigers had already offered Johnson a contract, so Evans had no choice but to opt for Averill instead. It was just one of those fluke chances that paid off.)

2. Tigers ace Earl Whitehill

3. .332

4. He hit four home runs during the twin bill, and collected 11 RBIs.

5. 32 in 1931 and 1932

6. Boston Red Sox

7. 1936

8. He played in 673 straight games.

9. A firecracker exploded in his hand and burned his thumb and two fingers. He was out for two weeks.

10. 1940

11. He went 0-for-3 in a pinch-hitting role.

12. Pitcher Harry Eisenstat (He won 10 games with Cleveland in 1939-42.)

13. Boston Braves (He played in only eight games with them.)

14. Yes (Earl Averill, Jr. saw limited action with the Tribe in 1956 and '58.)

15. He told them to decline the honor. Averill died on August 16, 1983.

4 - Bob Feller

1. He signed for one dollar.

2. Detroit Tigers

3. St. Louis Browns

4. He K'd 15 Browns during a 4-1 Tribe victory.

5. a.) 1938 b.) 240 strikeouts

6. Seven

7. 348 in 1946

8. 208 in 1938

9. U.S.S *Alabama*

10. Eight

11. Six

12. Six

13. Three no-hitters and 12 one-hitters.

14. Baseball's greatest living right-handed pitcher

15. The 1-0 loss to the Boston Braves in the first game of the 1948 World Series.

5 - Lou Boudreau
1. Thornton High School in Harvey, Illinois
2. Third base
3. Chicago White Sox
4. He received a $1,000 signing bonus and $100 a month for his mother while he attended college, and an extra $2,500 following his 60th major league game.
5. Since he was under contract, Boudreau was considered to be a pro ball player, which meant, of course, that he no longer had the status of an amateur.
6. He wanted to become a basketball coach.
7. George Martin
8. Lou hit .327 in 1944 to pace the league.
9. .978 (He broke the record in '47 with a .982 percentage.)
10. 134
11. He became the only AL player to have five extra-base hits in a game by cranking out a home run and four doubles.
12. St. Louis Browns.
13. Three ('41, '44 and '47)
14. Eight
15. .973
16. The Boston Red Sox in 1952-54, the Kansas City Athletics in 1955-57 and the Chicago Cubs for most of the 1960 season.
17. 1,162 wins and 1,224 losses
18. Ted Williams (The strategy was later re-named "The Williams Shift.")
19. *Good Infield Play* (He also co-authored a book titled, *Player-*

Manager.)
20. Denny McLain

6 - Bob Lemon
1. He was paid $100 a month, as well as a $500 signing bonus.
2. A Model-T Ford
3. He had one hit in nine at bats.
4. Two
5. Two
6. Seven
7. Three
8. Five
9. Four
10. a.) 350
b.) 188
c.) 31
11. a.) 2,850
b.) 1,277
c.) 1,251
12. .232
13. Three (1948, 1950 and 1954)
14. Kansas City Royals, Chicago White Sox and New York Yankees
15. a.) 1971 with the KC Royals and 1977 with the White Sox
b.) 1978 with the Yankees

V - MODERN STARS

1 - Albert Belle
1. a.) He was born in Shreveport, Los Angeles.
b.) Albert Jojuan Belle
2. Louisiana State University
3. In both seasons, he hit 21 HRs.
4. Seven
5. Nolan Ryan
6. Right field
7. 28

8. 129
9. He collected more than 100 extra base hits.
10. Eight (Mo Vaughn received 308 votes to Belle's 300.)

2 - Kenny Lofton
1. Arizona Wildcats
2. Point guard
3. Dick Vitale's "Dunk of the Year" Award
4. Five
5. 19
6. Milwaukee's Pat Listach
7. 66
8. 1993
9. He was named "Fastest Baserunner", "Best Bunter" and "Most Exciting Player."
10. Stolen bases (54) and triples (13)

3 - Charles Nagy
1. Roger Ludlowe High School in Fairfield, Connecticut
2. Football, basketball and baseball
3. University of Connecticut
4. He was named All-Big East Pitcher of the Year twice and made it on the All-New England Team twice.
5. He was the 17th overall player chosen.
6. He started 33 games and pitched 211.1 innings, the most by an AL rookie.
7. He was the first AL pitcher since 1963 to get a hit in the All-Star game.

8. 2.96
9. 4.55
10. a.) 17 wins
b.) .341 ERA

4 - Manny Ramirez
1. Manuel Aristides Ramirez
2. George Washington High School (New York City)
3. Three (1989, 1990 and 1991)
4. He was the 13th overall selection in the draft.
5. New York City Public Schools' "High School Player of the Year"
6. Minor League Player of the Year
7. The Yankees' Melido Perez
8. Kansas City's Bob Hamelin
9. He was the first Tribe hitter under 23 years of age to hit 30 or more home runs and collect more than 100 RBIs in a season.
10. a.) 33
b.) 112

VI - ODDS AND ENDS

1 - Trades and Acquisitions
1. New York Yankees
2. Baltimore Orioles
3. Len Barker and Bobby Bonds (From the Texas Rangers)
4. Pitcher Al Gettel and outfielder Hal Peck (Gettel was traded the next year, and Peck became a decent pinch-hitter after his first season on the team.)
5. Toby Harrah
6. Catcher Rick Cerone and

outfielder John Lowenstein
7. The Indians traded pitcher Tommy John, outfielder Tommie Agee and catcher John Romano to the White Sox for Colavito and catcher Camilo Carreon.
8. Washington Senators
9. Jim Busby and Chico Carrasquel
10. Chicago White Sox
11. Pedro Guerrero
12. Gale Wade (outfielder), Sam Jones (pitcher) and $60,000
13. Roger Maris
14. Pitcher Gaylord Perry and shortstop Frank Duffy
15. Philadelphia Athletics
16. Minnesota Twins
17. Jose Cardenal
18. Elmer Smith (outfielder)
19. Minnesota Twins
20. Minnie Minoso and Fred Hatfield (The Sox also received outfielder Al Smith in the deal.)

2 - Team Records
1. Mel Harder (582 games)
2. Bob Feller (3,827 innings)
3. Bob Feller (266 wins)
4. Mel Harder (186 defeats)
5. Feller (279)
6. Addie Joss (45)
7. Feller (2,581)
8. a.) Addie Joss
b.) 1.89
9. Jim Bagby, Sr. (31 victories in 1920)
10. a.) Joss
b.) 1.16 in 1908
11. Feller (348 in 1946)
12. 36

13. a.) 371
b.) 1946
14. Coveleski set a club record for most innings pitched in one day with 19.
15. He gave up 23 hits, which is the club record for most hits allowed in one game.
16. Terry Turner (1,619 games played)
17. 1,103
18. Nap Lajoie
19. Lajoie (2,051)
20. Tris Speaker
21. 242
22. Earl Averill
23. Averill
24. Kenny Lofton
25. Joe Jackson (.408 in 1911)
26. Jackson (233 in 1911)
27. 64
28. Hal Trosky
29. Burnett set the record for most at-bats in a game with 11, and for most hits in a game with nine. (It was an 18-inning game.)
30. Luke Easter (It was a 477-foot shot.)

3 - Milestones and Awards
1. Nap Lajoie (.344 in 1903)
2. Charlie Hickman (He had 193 hits in 1902.)
3. Seven (He hit three of them with the White Sox earlier in the season.)
4. Lajoie (102 in 1904)
5. Harry Bay
6. Earl Moore (1.74 in 1903)
7. Bill Bernhard (23 in 1904)
8. He won his 500th major league

game.

9. With a win over the Detroit Tigers Phil, along with his brother Joe, became the winningest brother combination in major league history. It was Phil's 314th victory and the Niekros' 530th.

10. Neal Ball (He played shortstop.)

11. He became the first player in franchise history to hit for the cycle.

12. He hit the first pinch hit grand slam in major league history.

13. The first AL night game was played on May 16, 1939. Cleveland beat the Philadelphia A's, 8-3, in 10 innings.

14. Herb Score (1955)

15. Joe Charboneau

16. First baseman Vic Power

17. Omar Vizquel (1994)

18. Andre Thornton

19. Gaylord Perry

20. Al Rosen

4 - At the Movies

1. Gene Bearden

2. *The Kid From Cleveland*

3. Bob Lemon (Ronald Reagan starred as Grover Cleveland Alexander in the picture.)

4. He played the role of Sergeant Sutton.

5. Johnny Beradino (He was known as Johnny Berardino when he played baseball, including three seasons with the Tribe.)

6. Leon Wagner

7. Leon Wagner

8. Michael Douglas

9. Bob Feller

10. *Don't Look Back*

5 - Broadcasters

1. Van Patrick

2. WEWS

3. One (1949)

4. Seven and a half (June 28, 1946-1953)

5. Ken Coleman

6. Chicago Cubs

7. Herb Score

8. 1968

9. Rocky Colavito

10. Rick Manning

6 - Important Games

1. Boston Red Sox (Cleveland won, 4-3)

2. The AL All-Stars (It was a benefit game for the family of Addie Joss following the pitcher's death. The Naps lost, 5-3.)

3. Cleveland beat St. Louis, 21-14.

4. a.) 24 b.) Indians won, 24-6

5. Lefty Grove

6. It was the first night game played in Cleveland Stadium. The Indians beat the Tigers, 5-0.

7. Feller threw a nine inning complete game for a 4-2 victory.

8. Ted Williams hit an inside-the-park home run to defeat Cleveland, 1-0.

9. Larry Doby made his major league debut, as a pinch-hitter vs. the Chicago White Sox. He struck out, but it was not an omen of things to come. (Cleveland lost the game, 6-5.)

10. Baltimore Orioles
11. Woodie Held, Pedro Ramos, Tito Francona and Larry Brown (The Indians won, 9-5, over the California Angels.)
12. Gaylord Perry pitched for the Tribe against his brother Jim, who started for the Tigers. Detroit won the game 5-4, with Gaylord taking the loss. Jim did not factor in on the decision.
13. Frank Robinson hit a home run in his first plate appearance as the Indians player/manager. Cleveland defeated the Yankees, 5-3.
14. 22 innings (Minnesota won, 5-4.)
15. It was the final Indians game played at Cleveland Stadium.

7 - Final Exam
1. 1901
2. The Cleveland Blues
3. Napoleon Lajoie
4. 1915
5. Louis Sockalexis (the first American Indian to play in Major League Baseball)
6. League Park, Cleveland Stadium (or Municipal Stadium) and Jacobs Field
7. a.) Two b.) 1920 and 1948
8. 111 wins in 1954
9. Rocky Colavito
10. Richard and David Jacobs

About the Author

Marc Davis was born in Conneaut, Ohio, but grew up in Oshkosh, Wisconsin, where he lives today. In between, he has lived for brief periods in Kingsville, Ohio; Nashua, New Hampshire; Lawrence, Massachusetts; Rockland Maine; and Oklahoma City, Oklahoma. *Cleveland Indians Facts & Trivia* is his second book. His first book was *Detroit Lions Facts & Trivia.*

His personal interests include collecting books and movies—classics as well as current releases—and he is an avid sports fan. In the summer, he lives out his "dream" of playing baseball. Not in the major leagues, of course, but on a local softball team.

Marc and his brother share a residence with their two dogs, Vixie and Noah. He works as a superviser for a major grocery store, and he works part-time at his father's flying school in Oshkosh.

AUTOGRAPHS

AUTOGRAPHS